How to Write a
Low-Cost/No-Cost Curriculum
for Your Home-School Child

— Also by Borg Hendrickson—

Home School: Taking the First Step
THE COMPLETE HOME-SCHOOL
PROGRAM PLANNING GUIDE
REVISED EDITION

"...**one of the primary references** for homeschoolers and those contemplating homeschooling."—North Carolina, *Families Learning Together*

"With Hendrickson's **clear and thorough guidance**, confusion and ignorance will melt and clarity of purpose will bloom...**Even if you've read them all, this book will aid and enlighten you** to a degree that few others do."—the *Grapevine*, Montana Home-School News

"<u>**Home School: Taking the First Step** is the book all parents need</u>... The book's step-by-step approach is **excellent**."
— *Library Journal*

"...a **comprehensive**...planning guide [which] pays great attention to detail [in a] **thorough but friendly** manner."—*Home Education Magazine*

"Borg Hendrickson brings you the first **step-by-step** guide to homeschooling!"
— *Hugs for the Heart*

"One of the **most thorough** resources available..."
—Hewitt Research Foundation

"*Home School: Taking the First Step* provides the reader with **a wealth of information**."
— *Family Learning Exchange*

"...a resource **to be referred to again and again**."
—*Oklahoma HERO News*

"...concise information...a **very user-friendly** publication.
—*CHEV Notes*

No book has more clearly and comprehensively laid the route to the home-school alternative — legal procedures, dealing with school officials, socialization, motivation, statements of intent, annual evaluation and other assessments, curriculum planning and materials, lesson planning, schedules and calendars, record keeping, support groups and services, readings and resources, teaching methods and keys to effective teaching. 337 information-packed pages for just $16.95.

Mountain Meadow Press

How to Write a
Low-Cost/No-Cost Curriculum
for Your Home-School Child

by

Borg Hendrickson

Mountain Meadow Press

How to Write a Low-Cost/No-Cost Curriculum for Your Home-School Child
by Borg Hendrickson

Cover Design by Jackie Holmes-Courtney

Published by Mountain Meadow Press
P. O. Box 318
Sitka AK 99835-0318
907/747-1026

© 1995 by Borg Hendrickson

Fourth Printing
REVISED EDITION
Printed in the United States of America

Hendrickson, Borg.
    How to write a low-cost/no-cost curriculum for your home-school child / Borg Hendrickson. -- Rev. ed.
    p. cm.
    Includes bibliographical references and index.
    ISBN 0-945519-21-4

    1. Home schooling--United States--Curricula.   I. Title.

LC40.H46 1995   649'.68
                                 QB195-20294

TABLE OF CONTENTS

NOTE: Feminine and masculine references are herein intermixed with no bias intended. Interpretations of state statutes are those of a layperson and do not constitute legal advice.

Introduction

YOUR MONEY OR YOUR TIME!

Imagine you are a determined home schooler ready to begin plans for the upcoming home-school year when a stranger stops by and offers to help you obtain a curriculum. This stranger, like the classical door-to-door salesperson, boldly states:

This curriculum will prove to be a reliable guide to your home-school program for the year.

This curriculum will help you establish a sound record of the educational journey your child will take.

This curriculum will be a valuable document should you ever face a challenge to your right to educate your child at home.

But these, you discover, are minor points, for with one polished shoe planted firmly on your doorsill, this stranger continues:

This curriculum will be easy to follow.

All of your child's educational interests, abilities, and needs can be covered in this curriculum.

You will know this curriculum intimately from the outset.

All of your own philosophies and aims for your child's education can be integral to this curriculum.

This curriculum will flexibly allow for your child's learning style and your own teaching style.

You may use whatever materials you wish, and even no materials when you wish, as you and your child work from this curriculum.

Then as a final *piece de resistance*, with smiles and excitement and one hand firmly gripping your doorframe, this seemingly sane stranger adds:

And...this curriculum is free!

As your mouth drops open and your widened eyes blink, you'll very likely reply with both eagerness and skepticism, "Uh huh? How?"

This book intends to show you how.

Through *How to Write a Low-Cost/No-Cost Curriculum for Your Home-School Child* you will develop a home-school curriculum which is reliable as a guide; a sound permanent record; acceptable to school officials; a useful court document; easy to use; intimately understandable; flexible; based upon your child's interests, abilities, and needs; instilled with your philosophies and aims; and free (or at least inexpensive). But there is a trade-off: Your time for your money. Yes, instead of writing checks for mail order curriculums written by people who don't know your child's individual needs and interests, you will have to expend some time to write your own curriculum. Not tremendous amounts of time, but a few days' effort will probably be necessary. This book will lead the way, step-by-step ...with no stall-outs.

Can you really do it? Can you actually create and write your own home-school curriculum? Yes, you can. And you should. Why?

You already intend to teach your children at home, an educational boon in itself, but whose curriculum will you teach? Integral to every curriculum (home-school or otherwise) are the values, beliefs, aims, objectives, and instructional methods of the framers of the curriculum. If you elect to use, for example, a commercial curriculum, or the scope and sequence of a textbook series, a private school curriculum, or your state's public school curriculum, you will be giving over the educational philosophies, lifelong learning aims, lesson objectives, and perhaps modes of teaching and selection of materials to the educators who wrote those curriculums. While you may obtain soundly written curriculums, perhaps useful as references, they will not be your own. They can not truly, fully reflect your educational intentions nor your child's educational needs or desires.

When I recently asked a home-school acquaintance of mine what she used for a curriculum, she replied, "Oh, Glenn, Oak Meadow, Davis, McGuffey, and the state music curriculum." In actuality, she had not one, but five curriculums, unrelated to each other, all designed by different people with different educational viewpoints, and while perhaps creditable in themselves, none of the five was *her* curriculum.

What other choice does she, and do you, have? You can opt to design and write your own curriculum — a true companion to your efforts to remove your children from the *system's* concept of what should be taught — and cradle your child in the relevancy of what you and he or she considers to be real and meaningful learning. While admittedly you'll probably need to meet state curricular requirements, want to include basic literacy goals, and hope to develop legally acceptable curriculum content and form, you have much more freedom and ability to create your child's curriculum than you may now think. And the only price is a measure of time.

How to Write a Low-Cost/No-Cost Curriculum for Your Home-School Child will first take you through the important step of identifying your educational philosophies and the long-term aims of your child's education; and then on to recognizing your child's learning interests, abilities, needs and style; to deciding which subjects to teach; to understanding the sequential nature of a curriculum and the format in which a curriculum is framed; and finally to writing your curriculum. Plenty of examples, useful worksheets, and suggestions for securing any needed assistance will help you along the way.

While your written curriculum will itself become a record of your child's educational experience at home, HOW TO WRITE A LOW-COST/NO-COST CURRICULUM FOR YOUR HOME-SCHOOL CHILD will further show you how to support your curriculum with other kinds of records that virtually prove that your child has followed a sound at-home curriculum.

Next you'll discover how to translate your curriculum into daily lessons which are as structured or unstructured as you wish. You'll also see how your curricular areas can be integrated into one another during lessons and how socialization can become an integral part of each subject area even though socialization is not itself a subject area.

Finally, this book will show you how next year's curriculum can be even freer than this year's. You'll discover that your first self-written curriculum may be used as a baseline from which you can design the following year's curriculum. In other words, each year your curriculum-writing experience will be easier than the last...and less costly, in terms of time. And each year, of course, it will remain low-cost or no-cost, in terms of dollars.

A forewarning: If you follow all the steps included in this book, you will write a well-structured curriculum for your child — complete with philosophies, lifelong aims, general learning goals and learning objectives. It will look professional; it will be exceptionally useable; yet it will allow you all the teaching flexibility you want. However, should you be one who stringently opposes including objectives in your curriculum, you may elect to complete only selected steps in the curriculum-writing process; that is, to use only those portions of this book that complement your own beliefs regarding the depth and structure of a desirable curriculum. You may, for example, want to include just philosophies, aims, and general learning goals. In that case, you could skim over those portions of the one chapter of this book which explains how to write learning objectives, but carefully read and complete all the other sections. As throughout this book, the choices are yours!

We'll begin, then, where all curriculums should begin: with *your* educational philosophies and *your* long-term aims for your child's education. These are perhaps the lowest-cost and yet richest elements of your home-written curriculum, and they already exist... within you. We just need to pull them out. Let's do that now — *freely*.

Borg Hendrickson

1

EDUCATIONAL PHILOSOPHIES AND LIFELONG AIMS
Did You Even Know You Had Them?

One of the reasons you have resisted public education is that you have deep, undeniable educational philosophies and aims related to your child's learning. While many think of philosophies and aims as just another example of professionalese (an affliction of the *experts*) or as educational gobbledygook, in actuality parents, too, have education-related philosophies and aims. However, many parents ignore these important elements of parental self-guidance, which is the same as ignoring themselves. Some parents begrudgingly abandon their philosophies and aims by letting them be overridden by those of the public school. More informed parents work with the public schools in an attempt to actualize at least some of the parents' own educational philosophies and aims within the school setting. The home-school parent, however, with greater self-affirmation, listens. She listens to her inner voice, the voice she recognizes as the world's most natural and suitable teacher for her children. She listens to her own convictions, to her life-earned wisdom, to her love for her children, to her hopes for them, and she then knows *how and to what purposes she wants her children educated.* She then knows her educational philosophies and aims. She also knows that nothing less will do.

Your first task, then, is to listen. How and to what purposes do you want your child educated? That is, what are your educational philosophies and long-term aims?

Let's begin with your philosophies. First, what do you hope your child's **learning attitude** will be? Acceptance of basics? Continual curiosity and seeking of knowledge? Inventiveness? Ongoing appreciation for and pleasure in the arts? A desire to share learning and contribute eventually to the development of knowledge in her own children and others? An eagerness to add knowledge to a particular field? A respect for the lessons of our historical past? What else?

Second, towards what **lifestyle** do you believe your child's learning should lead? Rural? Urban? Formal? Informal? Physically active? Industrious? Informed and involved? Creative? Artistic? A life of leadership? A Christian life? What other elements of lifestyle? Third, what **basic values** do you feel should be integrated into your child's curriculum? Honesty? Respect for others? Loyalty to family and friends? Generosity? A strong sense of the work ethic? Kindliness? What other values?

Next, **how** do you believe **children learn best**? By rote learning? Through manipulatives? Through hands-on experiences? Through reading and writing? With textbooks and workbooks? Alone? With peers? With a wide range of other persons? By watching? With a varying blend of the above? Or in yet other ways? Then, **how** do you believe **teachers teach best**? By lecturing? By assigning tasks and then staying out of the child's way until "correction" time? Through much interaction with the child? By offering much side-by-side assistance? By providing the structure within which a child may study, explore, experiment, and achieve? By modeling? How else?

Use a copy of Worksheet 1, "My Educational Philosophies," on page 7 to record your answers to these questions; i.e., your philosophies. Fill in each set of response lines even if you begin to feel that you are at times repeating yourself. Let all your thoughts flow onto the paper.

Finally, as an outgrowth and expansion of your educational philosophies, think and listen to yourself further. What do you believe should be the **lifelong learning aims** of your child's education? These will overlap with and stem from several of the above items. For example, by the time your child reaches adulthood, do you hope she will be self-reliant? Have the ability to think analytically? Live according to strong moral self-guides? Value a healthy environment? Be patriotic? Be physically fit? Be college educated? Be occupationally secure? What else? To further stimulate your thinking regarding aims, read through "Samples of Lifelong Educational Aims," on page 8. You may share some, even many, of these aims, and will undoubtedly have others of your own.

There are dozens of possible lifelong educational aims for a child's learning, as well as a wide variety of possible educational philosophies. No curriculum should be designed for use with your child until you have established in writing your own educational philosophies and aims for your child's education. All else that you include in your curriculum, and the manner in which you create lessons to teach it, stem from and are guided by these critical elements.

Now move ahead to Worksheet 2, "Lifelong Aims of My Child's Education," on page 9, where you will state long-term aims for your child's learning. Some entries will be repetitious of ideas written on Worksheet 1, some will stem from those ideas, and some will be new. Write them all. You may make as many copies of these worksheets as you wish for your own use. In fact, you may want at the outset to make copies of all the pages you will need for use with this book. To do so, turn to "Pages to Photocopy" on page 167.

Worksheet 1
My Educational Philosophies

1. I believe my child's learning attitude should be:

2. I believe my child's learning should lead towards this kind of lifestyle:

3. I believe the following basic values should be integrated into my child's curriculum:

4. How I believe children learn best:

5. How I believe teachers teach best:

6. My other educational philosophies:

Use photocopy master.

Samples of Lifelong Educational Aims

My child's curriculum year-by-year should enable him or her to:

Acquire no less than survival literacy

Examine and use information

Think analytically

Maintain a strong sense of self-worth

Be an informed citizen

Cooperate with others

Recognize his place in the brotherhood of mankind

Establish strong moral self-guides

Place God at life's center

Understand and respect cultural differences

Be self-reliant

Perceive and respect excellence

Function successfully in America's free enterprise system

Value a healthy environment

Compete well in the world of occupations

Gain a full, usable knowledge of English, reading, history, mathematics, science

Become college educated

Appreciate music, art, literature

Question authority

Be inventive

Be creative

Be physically fit and healthy

Be patriotic

Maintain a healthy relationship with a spouse

Others?

Worksheet 2
Lifelong Aims of My Child's Education

My child's curriculum year-by-year should enable him or her to:

1. _____

2. _____

3. _____

4. _____

5. _____

6. _____

7. _____

8. _____

9. _____

10. _____

11. _____

12. _____

13. _____

14. _____

15. _____

16. _____

17. _____

18. _____

Use photocopy master.

Now step back, look over your completed worksheets, let them sit for a day if you like, then begin weighing the most important against the least important. If you're married, you'll likely want to involve your spouse in this process. What if you and your spouse had to hone each list of philosophies and aims down to half of those you now have written? Which ones must be kept? Which could be crossed out? (Not erased!) Could some be combined? Or are you satisfied with all of them, just as they are?

When you have sufficiently mulled over the contents of your completed worksheets, write a *file copy*, a semi-finished statement of your philosophies and aims, on File Copy A, "My Educational Philosophies and the Lifelong Aims of My Child's Education" on page 11. The philosophies portion should appear in paragraph form, indeed as a statement. The aims may be listed. With this, then, you will have the first segment of your curriculum completed.

What you have written on File Copy A will slant some of the content of your curriculum. For example, you may select subjects to teach, subject area learning goals, lesson activities, materials and teaching aids based upon your philosophies and long-term aims. If some of your philosophies and aims are religion related, for instance, you are likely to design your curriculum and your daily lessons based upon religious principles, religious living and ideology, and religious models. You are also likely to select at least some if not most materials and teaching aids that are religion-based. A focus on religion will pervade any curricular area you cover. If, for another example, you are an environmentalist, much of your teaching of science may espouse a conservationist viewpoint — an understanding of conservation being a long-term educational aim in any curriculum you might design. You may further include that slant in your reading curriculum by including lesson objectives that would allow for stories and nonfiction about nature and environmental issues, and biographies of environmentalists. Creative writing objectives might involve nature writing and experiences in the natural world in preparation for writing compositions. Music curriculum objectives could aim to develop a recognition and appreciation of the sounds of nature. No commercial curriculum, textbook scope and sequence, nor public school curriculum would integrate your conservation-related long-term aim into the entire range of subject areas you will teach. By designing your own curriculum, you can do just that.

So keep in mind the importance and pervasive nature of your educational philosophies and lifelong aims for your child's education as you complete File Copy A and ready yourself for the next step, taking a look at your child as a learner.

File Copy A

My Educational Philosophies and the Lifelong Aims of My Child's Education

Statement of My Educational Philosophies:

_____
_____
_____
_____
_____
_____
_____
_____
_____
_____

Lifelong Aims of My Child's Education:

1. _____
2. _____
3. _____
4. _____
5. _____
6. _____
7. _____
8. _____
9. _____
10. _____
11. _____
12. _____

Use photocopy master.

2

YOUR CHILD
Uniqueness Personified

N ow that you have established in writing your own philosophies and the lifelong aims of your child's education, you must set yourself aside for a moment and consider that all-important person, your child. Just as no curriculum should be designed for your child which doesn't take into account your philosophies and aims, none should be designed which does not exhibit a sensitivity to who your child is.

State regulations seldom make mention of either you or your child, as individual teacher and learner with unique personal qualities and modes of thought. Your state laws may, however, make one requirement regarding your child as an individual — that the courses you teach be age/grade-level appropriate. This requirement is likely to influence the depth of coverage and choice of materials and methods for your child's home education, but certainly does not dictate them, any more than it dictates the philosophical slant of your curriculum.

Besides, you would naturally, with no regulation by the state, be sensitive to your child's age/grade level, along with his interests, needs, abilities, and learning style. Although these latter four considerations are as important, or more important, than age/grade, they are not even mentioned in most states' home-school regulations. Nevertheless, you are free and wise to consider them. **Your child's age/grade, interests, needs, abilities, and learning style can and should influence the content and direction of the curriculum you design for him as much as your own philosophies and aims.** How? Let's take a look.

If your child is six, for example, you're not likely to include the events that led to the Viet Nam War in his curriculum. Likewise, if he's fifteen, you're not likely to use manipulative math toys as an aid to teaching him math. If your child loves music and hates artwork, you're likely to follow his interest with an emphasis on music, while art may be less consistently or fully covered in his curriculum. If your child is exceptionally verbal, it is likely that he will learn best through verbal means, rather than through manipulatives. His learning style — strongly verbal — will affect your choice of methods and materials to use with his curriculum. You would be wise to allow many opportunities for him to use his verbal abilities — and experience much success — while learning new curricular skills which are more troublesome for him. In other words, who your child is as a learner will guide much of the direction of his curriculum.

So who is your child? We want to look at his age, grade level, academic interests, learning needs, academic abilities, and learning style. To begin, using a photocopy of Worksheet 3, "My Child," on page 15, first write down your child's name, age, and birthdate.

Next, if he has previously attended public school, write down the grade level to which he would now be assigned. If he has not previously attended public school, base your determination of grade level upon his age (this will be most acceptable to "the officials" but will not restrict you as you design your child's curriculum). If your child has failed a grade and is therefore older than others at his public school grade level, you may want to assign him to the lower grade level. At any rate, don't fret over this issue, for grade level ought not to be as important as it seems to be to public school folks. For the sake of your records, however, you should record as best you can his grade level. Also, for yourself, make a note of how you determined his level.

Now think about your child's interests, particularly those that fall within the range of academics. One of his interests, for instance, may be building sand castles. That in itself is not academic. However, is he interested in the size, shape, density, weight, and so on, of the castles — in other words, mathematics? Does he, as another activity, love to hear stories of the Old West? Do people of the past fascinate him? In other words, is history his bent? In the realm of the fine arts, does he enjoy drawing or playing a tonette or plunking on the piano? Or is giving a grand theatrical production on an apple-box stage his favorite? Is he, in other words, interested in art, or music, or drama? Continue to think over the kinds of activities your child enjoys. Try to identify in them the academic area within which they fall. Some will be easy — perhaps, for instance, your child directly says, "I want to learn to read." Others will take some thought on your part. As you jot down his interests on Worksheet 3, be both general and specific. For example, write down both music (general) and piano (specific), if those are his interests. Later as you design your curriculum, music will become a subject area while the piano will be one teaching aid and perhaps the hub of his lessons in music. (As you work, keep in mind that this worksheet will not actually become a page in your curriculum. Worksheet 3, while essential in designing a curriculum, is really just for you.)

Now look at his strengths, his academic abilities. In which skill or knowledge areas does he demonstrates proficiency? Does he, for example, read at age five? Or read exceptionally well at whatever his age? Does he quickly perform math computations with high accuracy? Is he skillful with his hands? With his body? Is he nimble, athletic? Is he mechanical? Musical? Verbal? Artistic? Be more specific, too, if you wish. For example, you might write, "He is a skillful watercolor painter." rather than just "He is artistic." Or "She knows a great deal about measurement in the kitchen. She reads recipes, measures and cooks on her own." rather than "She is good in math."

Worksheet 3
My Child

Child's name _____ Age ____ Birthdate _____

Grade level _____ How I determined grade level:

My child's academic interests, both general and specific:

My child's academic abilities:

My child's special learning needs:

Any learner labels that have been attached to my child by school personnel:

How do school records describe my child's deficiencies, difficulties, special needs, and/or special talents:

My child's learning styles:

Use photocopy master.

Next consider any learning needs that are unique to your child. Does he, for example, have a sight difficulty, or hearing problem, or physical or mental disability? Are you aware of any academic deficiencies? Are there any skill or knowledge areas with which he has had especial difficulty? Has your child ever been labeled "learning disabled" by school personnel? If so, why? Or "mentally retarded?" Or "gifted/talented?" Jot down any needs related to his learning on Worksheet 3. Incidentally, you needn't personally accept labels such as "learning disabled," but if the label has been designated by school personnel, it will appear on your child's school records. In that case, you will be expected to heed his known learning needs as you plan his curriculum, and you should have records to demonstrate that you indeed did so. The curriculum itself is one such record. So carefully read any school records available to you — if deficiencies and difficulties are noted for your child, what are they? List any labels identifying deficiencies and reasons behind those labels at the bottom of Worksheet 3. Then when you reach Chapter Four in this book, you'll be reminded to address any special needs of your child in his curriculum.

Finally, think about your child's dominant learning styles. Children and adults alike respond best to learning environments and methods most attuned to the learner's strongest natural modes of learning. While there is no one consistent definition/explanation of learning styles, we can discuss those characteristics of your child's learning style which may be at least informally observed. Does your child, for example, enjoy learning through firsthand experience — with real objects, in real settings, involving physical interaction? Many children do. Home-school learning situations can more easily adapt to this learning style than any other school setting.

What else can you observe to uncover the secrets to your child's most motivating and effective learning styles? Is your child, for instance, production oriented? Does she like to create and complete projects? Does invention excite her? Does she seem to gain more from process than from end product? Does she enjoy reasoning? Following logical steps to reach an end? Does goal-setting help her become motivated? Does she love to talk, listen, discuss? Does she best remember information conveyed to her verbally? Are the reactions of others to her work important to her? Does she become more fully engaged in a learning situation which involves other people? Group work? Or is she a loner? Does she like to work on her own initiative? Is concentration easy for her — especially in quiet, uncrowded environments? Does she like to try out new ideas to see if they work? Does she get most excited about situations that arouse her emotions or for which she feels empathy? Is she musical? Does the "Alphabet Song" help her remember the ABC's? Does she like regular schedules, or great flexibility, or something in-between? Does she like to bounce her ideas off other people? Does she like rules and established guidelines? Does she like routine? Or does she prefer to set her own pace? Perhaps she likes variety and diversity? Does she love opportunities to exercise imagination? Does she seem to be a "thinker?" Is she stimulated by problem-solving situations? Does she like to follow hunches, curiosities, intuitions? Does she tend to dig in depth into a subject or prefer to learn the essentials and move on? Does she like to act first and reflect later? Or think first before trying the act? Does she like to know what is expected of her? Does she exhibit patience in long-process situations? Does she enjoy memory exercises? Does she like surprises or does she like to know what's ahead? What kinds of situations hold her attention? Are there some situations in which she becomes totally absorbed? In what kinds of situations is she most persistent? In what kinds of situations does she become most frustrated?

By informally observing your child and then answering questions like these, you can develop a rough composite of your child's learning style tendencies. In other words, you're likely to find favorites, those situations which motivate her most easily and hold her attention, and other situations for which her response is flat or resistant. Then you can concentrate on consistently designing learning situations which you've discovered do stimulate her.

Learning style is linked to curriculum design in that the curriculum should liberally allow for the child to learn through her most dominant modes of learning. The physically-oriented child, for example, will learn best through the use of real-life settings, manipulative learning tools, exploration, and hands-on experiences. The "thinker" child will become most motivated when he is able to apply his logic and ability to analyze and when there is order to the components of a learning situation, including the teaching. Other situations will deflate his interest. The child who is highly emotive, empathetic, and sensitive to others and his own need for positive interaction with others, will want to feel good about his teacher, the subject, the learning situation, and will become motivated by that feeling. In the absence of that feeling, he is likely to be uninterested. Some children, on the other hand, respond best to creative, imaginative, open-ended, often-changing, unstructured learning situations and to teaching that above all inspires. The highly verbal child, for a last example, will be most motivated by enthusiastic verbal input and exchanges.

You should understand, too, that all children are able to learn through all styles of learning, but the strength of one or two modes will override the others. Denied many opportunities to learn through his strongest styles, the child's overall learning progress will be slower and more meager than otherwise possible and his interest may wane. Because public schools emphasize the verbal and logical, for instance, many students are left behind on the continuum of educational progress. Their individual learning styles are either little accommodated or not accommodated at all.

You may want to take time to make more careful observations of your child as he simply experiences the world day-to-day. Try to note how he interacts with the world — seemingly ordinary interactions are actually a continuous reel of learning situations. What do you see as his interests, his abilities, his needs, his learning styles? Record your observations on Worksheet 3.

When completed, bring Worksheet 3, along with File Copy A, back to this book to begin Chapter Three, "Subjects/Courses."

3

SUBJECTS/COURSES
Requirements and Choices

You might ask at this point how your own philosophies, the life-long aims of your child's education, and your child's learning interests, needs, abilities, and style can define your home curriculum when you know your basic roster of courses is *required* by the state. The answer: easily. Usually states only require that a particular course or subject be taught. Depth, direction, philosophical slant, materials, and methods are not mandated.

One state, for instance, may require that music be taught. But that state will not mandate that piano be included or excluded, that vocal training be included or excluded, that rock music be included or excluded, that you teach or not teach by the Suzuki method, that your activities include or avoid attending operas, and so on. The entire scope and sequence and all of the materials and methods of the music curriculum for a child in that state may be outlined and/or chosen by the parent teacher.

Even if your curriculum must be age/grade appropriate for your child, and your child is advanced, you can design a curriculum that includes the expected age/grade items but which also goes beyond them. Oftentimes, too, what is more advanced in practice can be couched in curricular words and sentences which appear to be basic for the particular age/grade. For example, if your ten-year-old's experience with the guitar has led him early into playing classical guitar, the curricular objectives can nevertheless be stated in a basic manner: The student will be able to distinguish "classical" from popular music. That statement sounds age/grade appropriate and it speaks honestly to a valuable curricular objective. In practice, however, your child may go well beyond that basic level.

At any rate, as you begin considering which subjects to teach at home, you must first look at your state's requirements. Most states require home schoolers to teach no less than a three-course or five-course core curriculum. Core courses include reading, language arts, mathematics, and often social studies and science. In some states, other courses, too, are specified as "required." Also, while your state may delineate required core courses, it may further expect that a broader curriculum be offered — one that includes the core subjects plus other subjects of your choice. In all states, as long as you do teach the required subjects, you may, whether expected to or not, teach other subjects of your choice.

In all cases, the particular areas/levels of a subject included in a child's curriculum would depend upon the above-mentioned **age/grade appropriateness.** This means that areas or levels within a subject that are *typically taught* at each age/grade in the public schools are areas or levels you will be expected to cover in your home school. For example, a full course in algebra is typically not taught until ninth grade. If you were teaching a child at that grade level, you should then consider including algebra in your math coverage. Also the extent of your coverage of any one area will depend upon age/grade appropriateness. Kindergartners are, for instance, merely introduced to fractions — "sometimes objects can be broken into parts, whole, half, and one-fourth parts." It would not *typically* be *appropriate* with kindergartners to teach fractions to any greater extent than a mere introduction.

Further, each subject would be taught in a **sequential** or **sustained** or **cumulative** fashion; that is, at *gradually increasing levels of difficulty* as the grades progress. In other words, fractions would be introduced in kindergarten, more deliberately introduced in grade one, taught and more extensively worked with in grade two, expanded to include one-eighth, one-sixteenth, etc., and eventually used in numerical and word problems.

Let's preview now the state requirements. The section below titled "What the States Require" tells you which subjects are required in your state and whether or not you will eventually need to submit your written curriculum to school officials. Other curriculum-related information which may be of help to you is also noted. When you read the subject requirements in this section, think of them in terms of your child's age/grade. The specific coverage typically given to each subject at your child's age/grade is the requirement for your coverage of the subject. Later you can also refer to the "Typical Grade-Level Subjects" on p. 40 for further assistance in deciding what your coverage should include. In addition, for a high-school-age home schooler, you should plan now to secure a copy of your state's requirements for high school graduation. You may wish to include in your home curriculum those courses required for graduation in your state, even if your child will not formally graduate and receive a diploma.

Subject terms in the chart below are all inclusive. In other words, *language arts* includes all language arts areas, such as creative writing, spelling, English usage or grammar, vocabulary, and so on. Even though *reading* and *literature* are among the language arts, they are oftentimes listed separately in the regulations. *Social studies* includes various social studies areas; i.e., history, geography, government, citizenship, etc. *Science* includes such areas as machines, magnets, weather, plant life, animal life, geology, etc. *Math* includes such areas as measurement, weight, computation, and geometry. Sometimes computer literacy is included as a math area subject. In some states additional courses or subject areas beyond the core courses are required — such as health and physical education, the constitution and citizenship, fine arts, or drug awareness. Some states further require that the language of instruction be English.

What the States Require

Please note that the information included in the following section does *not* constitute legal advice. Secure copies of your own state's regulations either from the state department of education or from a home-school organization in your state. Read those regulations carefully and, if needed, get help from a fellow home schooler to interpret them. Base your own procedures upon those regulations. But, for the sake of a preview and of preplanning, you may in the interim rely on this section.

Do realize, too, that home-school regulations undergo change from time to time — monitor your state legislature and routinely consult with home-school organizations in your state regarding legislative activity and home-school procedures.

Also, you'll probably discover that home-school regulations and procedures are sometimes vague or confusing — even to the point of needing litigious clarification at times. Often areas of procedural confusion are simply mapped out over time by state department of education personnel, local school district officials, and home-school parents themselves. One of those areas, generally a nonregulatory area, involves the availability of state or local district curriculums as samples for home-school parent educators. In some states, no state curriculums exist, likewise in some districts. In other states, state curriculums do exist, but they are not made available to home schoolers. In some local districts, certified district personnel will use local public school curriculums to assist parent educators in developing home curriculums. And in some states, state and local curriculums exist and are willingly shared with home-schooling families, often either free or for the cost of printing and postage. As you will discover later in this chapter, such curriculums may become useful references as you prepare your home curriculum.

In preparation for the writing of this book, a survey was sent to each of the fifty state departments of education and the District of Columbia's Public Schools Office. The survey asked the respondents to note whether or not state or local curriculums were "made available" to home schoolers. The responses are noted below in Item 3 for each state. If the notes indicate that no curriculums are *made available*, this does not necessarily indicate that no curriculums *exist*. In this case, if you'd like to use a state or local curriculum as one of your samples while you write your own curriculum, check with practicing home schoolers in your area to determine whether an official curriculum does exist and if someone has a copy which you could borrow. Please realize that while you may use such a curriculum as a *sample*, you'll not be locking yourself into state mandates, either for curriculum content or daily lessons.

In "What the States Require" below:

Item 1 lists required subjects.

Item 2 indicates whether or not you must submit a written curriculum to school officials.

Item 3 indicates the availability of state and/or local school district curriculums which could be used as samples while you write your own curriculum. Some states make their curriculum guides available at low-cost to nonresidents as well as residents.

After previewing the requirements of your state in this section, turn to page 37 to continue your curriculum-writing process.

> 1. Which subjects are required?
> 2. Must I submit a written curriculum?
> 3. Curriculum samples and additional notes.

ALABAMA

1. Reading and all other language arts, math, physical education, health, history, science, and geography. The language of instruction must be English.

2. No, but you do need to submit a list of courses to the county board of education or the city superintendent on a form provided by your state department of education.

3. While state curriculums and, in some school districts, local curriculums do exist, they are not routinely made available to home schoolers.

ALASKA

1. If you are home schooling for non-religious reasons you must teach either state or school district correspondence courses, or provide an educational experience that "equally well serves" the student. Required subjects are reading and all other language arts, and math.

2. Only if you plan to function entirely on your own; then the local school board should review and approve your home-school proposal.

3. Subject area, K-12, state curriculum guides are available ($4 each for residents; $6 each for non-residents). Write to Educational Program Support, P.O. Box F, Juneau AK 99811-0500. (907)465-2841. K-12 correspondence courses and textbooks are made available on a loan basis by the Department of Education's Centralized Correspondence Study Office.

ARIZONA

1. Reading, grammar, math, social studies, and science.

2. No

3. Subject area, K-12 curriculum guides are available ($2.42-$5.01 each). Write to the Director, Curriculum and Assessment Planning, AZ Department of Education, 1535 W. Jefferson, Phoenix, AZ 85007. (602) 542-5031 Ask for a list of the available Arizona Essential Skills (which are the Arizona curriculum outlines) and an order form.

> 1. Which subjects are required?
> 2. Must I submit a written curriculum?
> 3. Curriculum samples and additional notes.

ARKANSAS

1. Reading, language arts, math, social studies, and science.

2. Yes, to the local school superintendent.

3. Subject area, K-12 state curriculum guides are available ($10/set). Write to the Special Projects Manager, Curriculum and Assessment, #4 State Capitol Mall, Little Rock AR 72201. (501) 682-4474

CALIFORNIA

1. All language arts areas, math, social sciences, fine arts, health, science, and physical education.

2. A list of courses only, to the local school superintendent.

3. If you wish, your children may engage in independent study through your local public school with the assistance of a certified supervisor who designs or helps you design a curriculum. Contact your state department of education and/or your local school district for information regarding this option. To purchase curriculum guides, write the Department of Education, 721 Capitol Mall, Room 524, Sacramento CA 95814. Request their "Selected Publications" catalog.

COLORADO

1. Communication skills (reading, writing, listening, speaking), math, history, civics, science, literature, and the U.S. Constitution.

2. No

3. According to state personnel, neither state nor local guides are made available to home schoolers.

CONNECTICUT

1. Reading and all other language arts, math, U.S. history and government, local and state government, geography, and citizenship.

2. A written curriculum *may* be requested by the local school superintendent and subsequently presented to the local school board for approval.

3. Some local school districts share curriculum guides with home schoolers who request them.

---

1. Which subjects are required?
2. Must I submit a written curriculum?
3. Curriculum samples and additional notes.

DELAWARE

1. According to procedural guidelines, subjects taught in home schools should be the "same as public schools." Include no less than reading and all other language arts, and math.

2. No

3. While state and local curriculum guides do exist, according to state personnel those guides are not made available to home schoolers.

FLORIDA

1. "Sequentially progressive instruction" in no less than reading, language arts, math, science, and social studies.

2. No, but a portfolio must be maintained which reflects and documents your child's studies and his/her use of textbooks.

3. While state curriculum guides are not made available to home schoolers, some local school districts do provide curriculums upon request. Also, state graduation and curricular requirements for all grades are made available through the Regional Educational Division, 1662 Twin Towers E., Atlanta GA 30334. (404) 656-2446

GEORGIA

1. Reading, language arts, math, science, and social studies.

2. No

3. While state curriculum guides are not made available to home schoolers, some local school districts do provide curriculums upon request.

HAWAII

1. *Elementary*: language arts, math, social studies, science, art, music, health, and physical education. *Secondary*: social studies, English, math, science, health, physical education, and guidance.

2. Yes, to the local school principal.

3. According to state personnel, neither state nor local guides are made available to home schoolers.

> 1. Which subjects are required?
> 2. Must I submit a written curriculum?
> 3. Curriculum samples and additional notes.

IDAHO

1. Reading, language arts, math, U.S. Constitution, use of the American flag, national colors, Pledge of Allegiance, the national anthem, the anthem "America," health, physical fitness, drug awareness, and Arbor Day from a preservation perspective.

2. No, but local school officials may request one.

3. According to state personnel, neither state nor local guides are made available to home schoolers.

ILLINOIS

1. According to procedural guidelines, home curriculums should be "equal to or superior to public schools." Reading, language arts, and math are specified. The language of instruction must be English.

2. No

3. According to department of education personnel, neither state nor local guides are made available to home schoolers.

INDIANA

1. According to procedural guidelines, home curriculums should include subjects "equivalent to public schools." Reading, language arts, math, science, and social studies are specified. The language of instruction must be English.

2. Submittal procedures vary by local school district. Check with practicing home schoolers within your school district to determine local practices.

3. While state curriculum guides are not made available, some local school districts do provide them to home schoolers upon request.

IOWA

1. *Grades 1-6*: reading and all other language arts, math, art, handwriting, health, physical education, music, science, social studies, traffic safety, and career education. *Grades 7-8*: reading and all other language arts, math, art, health, physical education, music, science, social studies, and career education. The language of instruction must be English.

2. If requested by local school district officials.

---

1. Which subjects are required?
    2. Must I submit a written curriculum?
        3. Curriculum samples and additional notes.

Iowa (continued)

3. Secure from your state department of education its "Equivalent Instruction Standards." Subject area state curriculum guides are available. Write to Chief, Bureau of Instruction and Curriculum, Iowa Department of Education, Grimes Bldg., Des Moines IA 50319-0146. (515) 281-4803

Kansas

1. Reading and all other language arts, math, government, history, geography, health, and science.

2. No

3. While state curriculum guides are not made available, some local school districts do provide guides to home schoolers upon request.

Kentucky

1. No less than reading, language arts, and math.

2. If requested by the local school superintendent.

3. According to department of education personnel, neither state nor local guides are made available to home schoolers.

Louisiana

1. According to procedural guidelines, home teachers must offer a "sustained curriculum at least equal to that of the public schools." Include no less than reading, language arts, math, social studies, and science.

2. You may elect to submit a written curriculum as part of your end-of-the-school-year documentation to show that you have provided a sustained curriculum. Ask your state department of education for a copy of its "Home Study Guidelines," which explains documentation options.

3. Subject area, K-12 state curriculum guides are available ($2 to $10.50 each). Write to the Louisiana Department of Education, Bureau of Secondary Education (Curriculum), P O Box 94064, Baton Rouge LA 70808. (504) 342-3404

> 1. Which subjects are required?
> 2. Must I submit a written curriculum?
> 3. Curriculum samples and additional notes.

MAINE

1. No less than reading and all other language arts, math, physical education, history/social studies, U.S. and Maine constitutions, and science.

2. Yes, to the local school superintendent.

3. Forms are available for recording your home-school syllabus and a description of your curricular program. Secure a copy of "Regulations and Guidelines for Equivalent Instruction Through Home Instruction" from a practicing home schooler, the Maine Homeschool Association, or your state department of education (Department of Educational and Cultural Services, State House Station #23, Augusta ME 04333).

MARYLAND

1. Reading and all other language arts, math, art, music, health, physical education, science, and social studies.

2. No, but your curriculum may be reviewed by public school officials at the end of each semester, and you should keep a portfolio which demonstrates your use of a "comparable" curriculum.

3. No state curriculum guides are available; some local districts make their guides available to home schoolers upon request.

MASSACHUSETTS

1. Reading and all other language arts, math, art, music, physical education, health, social studies, science, principles of "good behavior," and any other subjects required by the local school committee.

2. Yes, to your local school committee. If denied approval of your curriculum, ask for revision recommendations. You may then revise and submit it again.

3. While no state curriculum guides are made available, some local school districts do provide curriculums to home schoolers upon request.

MICHIGAN

1. According to procedural guidelines, home curriculums should be "comparable to those taught in the public schools," but should include no less than reading and all other language arts,

1. Which subjects are required?
2. Must I submit a written curriculum?
3. Curriculum samples and additional notes.

MICHIGAN (continued)

math, U.S. and Michigan constitutions and histories, the political subdivisions and municipalities of Michigan, social studies, and science.

2. No, but your at-home curriculum should be available for review at any time.

3. Subject area, K-12 curriculums are made available at no cost. Write to the Michigan Department of Education, Instructional Specialist Program, P O Box 30008, Lansing MI 48909. (517) 373-7248

MINNESOTA

1. Reading, math, writing, literature, fine arts, science, history, geography, government, health, physical education, citizenship.

2. No, but your at-home curriculum should be available for review at any time.

3. While no state curriculum guides are made available, some local districts do provide them to home schoolers upon request.

MISSISSIPPI

1. While procedural guidelines do not specify required subjects for home schoolers, you may be wise to include no less than reading, language arts, and math.

2. Yes, to your local school district attendance officer. Secure a *certificate of enrollment* form on which to record your educational plan and scope.

3. According to state personnel, neither state nor local curriculum guides are made available to home schoolers. However, you may attempt to secure a copy of the state department's "Curriculum Structure" manual, which is used by Mississippi public schools (Department of Education, 501 Sillers Bldg., Jackson MS 39201).

MISSOURI

1. Reading, language arts, math, science, and social studies.

2. No

3. According to state personnel, neither state nor local curriculum guides are made available to home schoolers.

---

1. Which subjects are required?
2. Must I submit a written curriculum?
3. Curriculum samples and additional notes.

MONTANA

1. "Subjects basic to the instructional programs of the public schools;" no less than reading and all other language arts, and math.

2. No

3. According to department of education officials, neither state nor local curriculum guides are made available to home schoolers.

NEBRASKA

1. Reading, language arts, math, health, science, social studies.

2. Yes, to the state commissioner of education.

3. According to department of education officials, neither state nor local curriculum guides are made available to home schoolers.

NEVADA

1. According to procedural guidelines, home schools should provide "equivalent instruction" to that offered in public schools. Reading, language arts, math, U.S. and Nevada constitutions, science, and social studies are specified.

2. Yes, to the local school superintendent.

3. While no state curriculum guides are made available, some local school districts do provide their curriculum guides to home schoolers upon request.

NEW HAMPSHIRE

1. Reading and all other language arts, math, history, government, U.S. and New Hampshire constitutions, geography, and music. Also physiology and hygiene as they relate to the effects of alcohol, other drugs, and venereal disease on the human system.

2. Yes, *if not* exempt from compulsory attendance laws for religious reasons.

3. Secure a copy of the booklet "Regulations and Procedures for Home Education Programs in New Hampshire" from your state department of education. State curriculums are available. Write to the Director, New Hampshire Department of Education, Standards and Certification, 101 Pleasant Street, Concord NH 03301. (603) 271-3453

1. Which subjects are required?
2. Must I submit a written curriculum?
3. Curriculum samples and additional notes.

NEW JERSEY

1. According to procedural guidelines, home curriculums should be "equivalent to public school." Include no less than reading, language arts, social studies, and math.

2. No, but your at-home curriculum must be available for review at any time.

3. No state curriculum guides are made available, but some local districts do provide them to home schoolers upon request.

NEW MEXICO

1. Reading, language arts, math, science, and social studies.

2. No

3. Secure a copy of "Minimum Standards" from the state department of education. Write Department of Education, Education Bldg., Santa Fe NM 87501-2786.

NEW YORK

1. No less than reading, language arts, math, physical education, science, and social studies.

2. If requested by local school officials.

3. Consult with practicing home schoolers in your school district. Secure a copy of the "Individualized Home Instruction Plan" form from the local school superintendent. Subject area, K-12 curriculum guides are available ($.25 to $4.50 each + $1.50 postage). Write for a copy of the current "Publications Catalog": New York State Education Department, Publications Sales Desk, Rm. 171 Education Bldg. Annex, Albany NY 12234.

NORTH CAROLINA

1. According to procedural guidelines, home curriculums should meet "such minimum curriculum standards as are required of public schools." Include no less than reading, spelling, grammar, English, music, Americanism, free enterprise, physical education, health.

2. No

3. According to state personnel, neither state nor local curriculums are made available to home schoolers.

> 1. Which subjects are required?
> 2. Must I submit a written curriculum?
> 3. Curriculum samples and additional notes.

NORTH DAKOTA

1. No less than reading, language arts, math, science, agricultural science, and social studies.

2. No, but you must maintain curricular records.

3. Subject area, K-12 state curriculum guides are made available to home schoolers upon request. Write to the Director, North Dakota Department of Public Instruction, 600 E. Boulevard, Bismarck, ND 58505-0440. (701) 224-2295 Some local district guides may also be available.

OHIO

1. Reading and all other language arts, math, science, geography, health, physical education, U.S. and Ohio history, U.S. and Ohio and local government, music and other fine arts, first aid, safety and fire prevention.

2. Yes, to the local school superintendent.

3. While no state curriculum guides are available, some local districts do make available their "Courses of Study" outlines upon request.

OKLAHOMA

1. According to procedural guidelines, home curriculums should be "equivalent to public schools." Include no less than reading and all other language arts, math, science, and social studies.

2. No

3. Subject area, K-12 state curriculum guides are available upon request. Write to the Executive Director, Curriculum; Oklahoma State Department of Education, 2500 North Lincoln Blvd., Oklahoma City OK 73105-4599. (405) 521-3361

OREGON

1. No less than reading and all other language arts, math, science, and social studies.

2. No

3. While no state curriculum guides are made available, some local school districts do make their guides available upon request.

> 1. Which subjects are required?
> 2. Must I submit a written curriculum?
> 3. Curriculum samples and additional notes.

PENNSYLVANIA

1. *Elementary*: reading, math, writing, spelling, English, geography, U.S. and Pennsylvania history, science, civics, loyalty to the state and national governments, safety, humane treatment of wildlife, health, physical education, physiology, music, and art. *Secondary*: English, math, art, health, music, physical education, science, social studies, U.S. and Pennsylvania history. The language of instruction must be English.

2. Yes, you will need to file an affidavit with the local school superintendent verifying, among other things, that you will teach the required subjects for the required number of hours. A complete curriculum outline must be attached.

3. While no state curriculum guides are made available, local school districts must provide their curriculum guides to home schoolers upon request.

RHODE ISLAND

1. No less than reading and writing, English, math, geography, U.S. and Rhode Island history, and the principles of American government. The language of instruction must be English.

2. Yes, to your local school superintendent or school committee.

3. Before contacting local school officials, consult with members of Parent Educators of Rhode Island (P O Box 546, Coventry RI 02816). You'll want to assess the home-schooling climate in your county before going public. While no state curriculum guides are made available, some local school districts do provide them to home schoolers upon request.

SOUTH CAROLINA

1. Reading, writing, math, social studies, science and, in grades 7-12, composition and literature.

2. Yes, to the local school board.

3. According to state personnel, neither state nor local curriculum guides are made available to home schoolers.

SOUTH DAKOTA

1. Reading, language arts, math, free enterprise, science, and social studies. English language mastery must be one of your child's curricular goals.

---

1. Which subjects are required?
2. Must I submit a written curriculum?
3. Curriculum samples and additional notes.

SOUTH DAKOTA (continued)

2. No

3. While no state curriculum guides are made available, some local school districts do make guides available to home schoolers upon request.

TENNESSEE

1. While procedural guidelines do not specify required subjects for grades K-6, you may be wise to include no less than reading, language arts, math, science, and social studies. Grades 9-12 home courses should include those required by the State Board of Education for graduation from Tennessee public schools.

2. Yes, to the local school superintendent.

3. According to state personnel, neither state nor local curriculum guides are made available to home schoolers. To secure graduation requirements, contact the local school superintendent or write to the Department of Education, 100 Cordell Hull Bldg., Nashville, TN 37219.

TEXAS

1. Reading, spelling, grammar, math, and good citizenship.

2. No, but your curriculum should be available for review at any time.

3. According to state personnel, neither state nor local curriculum guides are made available to home schoolers.

UTAH

1. Reading and all other language arts, math, science, social studies, fine arts, health, and computer literacy.

2. No, but proof of a satisfactory curriculum must be maintained, and a list of subjects being taught may be requested.

3. Secure a copy of "CORE Standards for Utah Public Schools" to determine acceptable curricula for your home school. Subject area, K-12 state curriculum guides are available to home schoolers upon request. Write to the Education Specialist, Utah State Office of Education, Operations Division, 250 East 500 South, Salt Lake City UT 84111

> 1. Which subjects are required?
> 2. Must I submit a written curriculum?
> 3. Curriculum samples and additional notes.

VERMONT

1. Reading and all other language arts (including English and American literature), math, health (including drug awareness), the natural sciences, physical education, social studies (including U.S. and Vermont history and government), and citizenship.

2. Yes, to your state department of education.

3. While curriculum guides *per se* are not made available to home schoolers, you may inquire at your local school district office about curricular "frameworks."

VIRGINIA

1. While specific courses are not required, your state's board of education "urges" home schoolers to include courses "comprehensive and comparable" to those of public schools in all the language arts, math, science, and social studies.

2. Yes, to the local school superintendent.

3. If you decide to enroll your children in a correspondence school, ask your state department of education for a copy of its approved "Correspondence Courses for Home Instruction." While no state curriculum guides exist, you may request the "Standards of Learning Objectives," which are available ($3) for grades K-12. Write to the Associate Director, Proprietary School Services, Virginia Department of Education, P.O. Box 60, Richmond VA 23216-2060.

WASHINGTON

1. Reading and all other language arts, math, health, occupational education, U.S. and Washington constitutions, science, social studies (including history), and art and music appreciation.

2. No, but curricular records must be maintained.

3. Your home courses may be approved for credit provided you submit to the local school district an acceptable proposal for such prior to course implementation. Your child may enroll part-time in courses or participate in ancillary services at the local public school. While no state curriculum guides are available, some local school districts will provide their district guides to home schoolers upon request.

> 1. Which subjects are required?
> 2. Must I submit a written curriculum?
> 3. Curriculum samples and additional notes.

WASHINGTON, D.C.

1. According to procedural guidelines, home curriculums should be equivalent to public schools. Include no less than reading and all other language arts, and math.

2. Only a list of courses, to the local school board.

3. K-12 District of Columbia curriculum guides are available at no cost. Write to the Assistant Superintendent, Curriculum Division, Twentieth & Evarts Streets NE, Washington DC 20018. (202) 576-6580. Local guides are also available.

WEST VIRGINIA

1. Reading, language arts, math, science and social studies.

2. Yes, to the county superintendent or school board.

3. Your county superintendent or a designee "shall offer" textbooks, other teaching materials and resources for your use. Your child may enroll in any class offered by the county board. According to state personnel, neither state nor local guides are made available to home schoolers.

WISCONSIN

1. Reading, language arts, math, health, science, social studies.

2. No

3. While no state curriculum guides are available, some local school districts provide guides to home schoolers upon request.

WYOMING

1. A "sequentially progressive curriculum" that includes reading, writing, math, civics, history, literature, and science.

2. Yes, to the local school board.

3. While state curriculum guides are not available, some local school districts provide guides to home schoolers upon request.

To supplement your reading of your state's requirements above, take time now to look at the "Typical Grade-level Subjects" roster on page 40. Remember, it is just *typical*, just a reference to help you think about your own coverage. In some states, the regulations state that you must teach courses "usually taught in public schools." The "Typical Grade-Level Subjects" roster is likely to correlate well with what is usually taught in your state's public schools. If required, you must include the locally taught courses in your child's curriculum. However, the extent to which you will teach them remains up to you.

As noted above, you may benefit throughout the entire process of writing your own curriculum from a few sample curriculums, not to be used wholesale, but only as references. Take time to search for and borrow sample curriculums for your child's age/grade. Besides local schools or school teachers and state departments of education, fellow home schoolers who use commercial curriculums and college libraries are likely sources.

Now take a look at Worksheet 4, "Requirements and Choices," on page 38. Refer to the above "What the States Require" chart to fill in the first column, "Required Subjects for Home Schoolers in My State."

When done, note the heading for column two: "Subjects I Noted in Sample Curriculums or in the Typical Grade-level Subjects" roster. For the sake of column two, you need to explore possibilities by reviewing your sample curriculums, the "Typical Grade-level Subjects" roster, and any needed information regarding local school course offerings. Then, list those subjects that appeal to you.

Next, spend a few minutes brainstorming subjects that you have wanted to teach your child or to which your child is particularly attracted or for which he seems particularly ready. Refer to File Copy A and Worksheet 3 for thought stimulators. Perhaps you'll elect to include conservation or environmental awareness, perhaps nutrition and health foods, or fine arts, or current affairs, or poetry writing, or auto mechanics, or .... Think also about your talents — what you can offer as a mentor/teacher. Think about your child's talents and interests. Write any additional subject possibilities that you think of in column three on Worksheet 4.

Finally, it's time to seriously mull over your Worksheet 4 lists. Ponder your possible subject areas until you can settle on those you must teach and those you additionally want to teach. Realize that not every subject need be taught all year long. Perhaps subjects like citizenship and safety, for example, will only be directly taught for six weeks and just practiced the rest of the year. When you've made your decisions, circle the chosen subjects on Worksheet 4, and then complete File Copy B, "My Child's Home-School Subjects" on page 39.

When you have completed File Copy B, take it, File Copy A, and Worksheet 3 with you to Chapter Four, "Goals and Objectives — The Stuff of Which Curriculums Are Made." You're ready for the next step in preparing your own low-cost/no-cost curriculum.

Worksheet 4
Requirements and Choices

Required Subjects for Home Schoolers in My State	Subjects I Noted in Sample Curriculums or in the "Typical Grade-Level Subjects" Roster	Other Subjects I Want to Teach or That My Child Wants to Study
_____	_____	_____
_____	_____	_____
_____	_____	_____
_____	_____	_____
_____	_____	_____
_____	_____	_____
_____	_____	_____
_____	_____	_____
_____	_____	_____
_____	_____	_____
_____	_____	_____
	_____	_____
		_____

Notes:

File Copy B

My Child's Home-School Subjects

1. _____

2. _____

3. _____

4. _____

5. _____

6. _____

7. _____

8. _____

9. _____

10. _____

11. _____

12. _____

13. _____

TYPICAL GRADE LEVEL SUBJECTS

The following rosters are only *typical.* If your state requires that you teach courses that are equivalent to those taught in the public schools, find out what courses are taught in your local schools. In the meantime, the rosters below can provide a preview of what you are likely to find as the locally taught courses. Beyond the inclusion of required courses in your home curriculum, the choices are yours!

Kindergarten Through Grade Six	Grades Six or Seven Through Eight	Grades Nine through Twelve
Reading	English (or Language Arts or Reading)	3-4 English courses
Language Arts		1-4 Math courses
Mathematics	Mathematics	1-4 Science courses
Science	Science	1-4 Physical education courses and health
Social Studies	Social Studies	
Music	Physical Education	A specified number of electives: fine arts courses, vocational courses, consumer courses
Art	Electives: music, art, home economics, industrial arts	
Physical Education		

NOTE: A rundown of general areas typically included in each of the above subjects is provided on pages 41-42.

General Coverage within the Typical Grade-Level Subjects

Kindergarten through grade six

reading — oral language activities, the alphabet, and phonics at the beginner levels; comprehension, fluency, leisure reading, children's literature, reading for information, oral storytelling

language arts — spelling, creative writing, English grammar, informal oral presentation or speech, handwriting, vocabulary development

math — patterns (e.g.: colors, sizes, shapes, groups of objects; especially at the beginner levels), the number system, basic geometry, measurement, mathematical computation, problem solving, possibly computers

science — the five physical senses, basic meteorology, basic botany and zoology, basic physics and chemistry, basic geology, environmental science, scientific tools and processes

social studies — U.S. and state history, basic sociology, cultural awareness, basic geography, basic civics, basic economics, citizenship

music — rhythm, vocal music, instrumental music, music reading, musical performance, music appreciation

art — the visual arts and crafts, color theory, design and art processes, art appreciation

physical education — body awareness and control, physical fitness, recreation, health and safety, possibly drug awareness, individual and team sports

Grade Six or Seven Through Eight

English — grammar, vocabulary, spelling, creative writing, literature, reading comprehension (The terms "language arts" and "reading" may still be used at this level.)

math — more advanced, but the same skill areas as K-6; possibly computers; possibly an introduction to algebra

science — more advanced, but the same knowledge areas as K-6

social studies — more advanced, but the same knowledge areas as K-6; possibly one selected social studies area, such as state history at grade 8

physical education — more advanced, but the same skill areas as K-6; probably more emphasis on sports, team play, strength and endurance training

music — more emphasis on practice and performance of instrumental or vocal music

art — more advanced practice of art skills

Grades Nine Through Twelve

English — Continued development of writing skills and vocabulary, building to college prep levels as desired. Grammar is practiced, sometimes just as need becomes apparent in connection with writing lessons. Literature becomes more prominent in the curriculum. Typically, at the junior level, American literature is studied; and at the senior level, British literature or world literature may be studied.

math — freshman math, algebra or an advanced general math; sometimes computers; sophomore math, algebra and/or geometry; junior math, typically advanced algebra; senior math, trigonometry and/or possibly basic calculus or other college prep math

science — freshman, earth science or biology; sophomore, biology or chemistry; junior/senior, chemistry and/or physics

social studies — American history, American government (often at grades 11 and 12 respectively); perhaps a global issues/current affairs course; perhaps economics or consumer education courses; perhaps introductory sociology, anthropology, or psychology

4

GOALS AND OBJECTIVES
The Stuff of Which Curriculums Are Made

Once you have completed the first three preparatory steps; that is,

1. stated your educational philosophies and the life-long aims of your child's education;
2. identified your child's learning interests, abilities, needs, and style; and
3. decided your subjects or courses;

— *you're ready to begin* —

4. writing your curriculum course-by-course.

Just how to form or frame your curriculum, in writing, is our next consideration. Sometimes curricular outlines are unassumingly simple, a one-page list of subjects, main focuses, and textbooks to be used. In truth, such is not a curriculum. If you hope to provide yourself with a complete guide to a year's home education for your child and to maintain a curriculum that would meet any official challenge, you need a more carefully and thoroughly written document. That means you need to write what educators call "goals and objectives" for each course.

Doing so is not difficult. To help you, lots of examples will be given below, but do keep your sample curriculums handy. (If you haven't secured any yet, take time to round some up now.) From them you can gain a further understanding of how your written curriculum might look when completed, how to phrase your goals and objectives, and which goals and objectives are commonly listed in your chosen subject areas. Let's look, then, at goals and objectives, the stuff of which curriculums are made.

With your first preparatory step in Chapter One, you listed educational aims for your child which are broad and hold lifelong applications. As you did so, you thought of these aims as if they were long-range targets towards which a series of learning experiences led. The goals of which we speak in this chapter are subject area learning goals. Subject area learning goals are likewise targets. However, as such, these targets are smaller in scope, more specific, and apply more narrowly to one subject at a time. They will remain the targets only for the duration of one year's course in each subject. They may, however, be reestablished as targets in the following year's curriculum, if appropriate, and will function from year to year as the building blocks of your child's long-term educational aims.

The objectives of which we speak in this chapter are subject area learning objectives, which step-by-step lead your home student toward his subject area goals. The objectives, in other words, are the immediate (hoped for) results of any lesson's learning activities (allowing, incidentally, that a lesson may extend beyond one or two days).

> For example, if today's learning activity for your home-school child involved a walk through the woods to identify tree species, the objective would be *to demonstrate his recognition of tree species by sight.*

> For a second example, if today's activity involved using a recipe to bake a batch of cookies, the objective might be *to accurately measure by teaspoons, tablespoons, and one-fourth, one-half, and full cups.*

> For a third example, if today's activity involved reading a story and discussing it aloud with you, the objectives might be *to identify the main character and minor characters in the story and to outline a plot sequence.*

Both learning goals and learning objectives are stated in terms of what the student will demonstrate she can do or has learned. In other words, the first objective example above would not be stated as "the student will know tree species," because that statement implies no *demonstration of knowledge* of species. The second would not be stated as "the student will bake cookies," because that statement implies no *demonstration of her skill* to measure accurately. The third would not be stated as "the student will read and discuss a story" when the true objective is that she *demonstrate her ability* to recognize main and minor characters and plot.

This may sound unnecessarily precise; however, you can only know if a child has learned something if that child *demonstrates* that she has learned it. Therefore, a complete curriculum identifies what specific skills and knowledge the child will demonstrate, and these are stated as learning objectives.

In review: For each subject, you will write learning goals. Under each learning goal, you will write learning objectives which are the steps your student must achieve in order to reach each goal. Both goals and objectives will be stated in terms of what your student will demonstrate she has achieved; that is, her skills and knowledge. Simple? Let's see ...

Consider this example:

Subject: **ART**

Goal 1: The student will be able to use basic art tools to explore and create artwork.

Objective 1.1: The student will be able to cut basic figures (circle, square, triangle, rectangle) with scissors.

Objective 1.2: The student will be able to paint what she considers an acceptable picture with water-paints and a paint brush.

Objective 1.3: The student will be able to use glue to piece together a 3-5 piece craft item.

Goal 2: The student will be able to experiment with and use colors for fun and effectiveness in artwork.

Objective 2.1: The student will be able to identify the three primary colors (red, yellow, blue) as the "primary colors."

Objective 2.2: The student will be able to identify the three secondary colors (purple, green, orange) as the "secondary colors."

Objective 2.3: The student will be able to recognize and name the six colors on the color wheel and black and white.

Objective 2.4: The student will be able to use the three primary colors to create a six-color color wheel.

Objective 2.5: When given paints in the primary colors, the student will be able to paint a picture which includes all six colors.

Objective 2.6: The student will be able to use black and white to change the value or tint of the primary and secondary colors.

Goal 3: The student will be able to recognize and create designs.

Objective 3.1: The student will be able to point out designs in nature as "designs."

Objective 3.2: The student will be able to make designs using various media of her choice.

For a kindergarten or first grade student, this example could comprise much of the art curriculum for a year. The activities you and she complete to achieve the above objectives may be many and varied, and while completing them, you may be as spontaneous as you like. Pleasure may pervade your lessons. But all the while, you will have a sound art curriculum as the basis of what you are doing.

Should you need to submit or maintain such a curriculum for inspection or in case of a legal challenge, or would you want a detailed guide, you will have in writing the document you need. And, yes, while it will take a little time to write, your curriculum will be reasonably simple. And most important, it will be thoroughly yours!

You no doubt noted the repetition of the phrase "The student will be able to..." at the beginnings of the goals and objectives statements in the above example. This phrase is standard. It appears in most curriculums used by public and private schools throughout the country. Therefore, you would be wise to use it if one of your purposes is to create an officially acceptable curriculum. However, you needn't write the standard opening phrase over and over as in the example. Instead you would write the phrase at the top of each list of goals and each list of objectives, as in the following example. Also note the numbering system: The goals are each assigned one number and consecutively arranged. The objectives are given two numbers, the first of which identifies the goal and the second of which identifies the objective, again consecutively arranged.

Subject: **ART**

Goals	**Objectives**
The student will be able to:	The student will be able to:
1. use basic art tools to explore and create artwork	1.1. cut basic figures with scissors.
	1.2. paint what she considers an acceptable picture with water paints and a paint brush.
	1.3. use glue to piece together a 3-5 piece craft item.
2. experiment with and use colors for fun and effectiveness in art work.	2.1. identify the three primary colors (red, yellow, blue) as the "primary colors"
	2.2. identify the three secondary colors (purple, green, orange) as the "secondary colors."

...and so on through the art curriculum.

Now that you know what subject area learning goals and learning objectives are and how to write them with the opening phrase "The student will be able to...", you must decide what goals and what objectives you want to include in your child's curriculum.

You already know two guidelines to help you decide what goals and objectives to include:

1. The goals and objectives must be age/grade appropriate for your child.

2. They must be arranged sequentially (most basic to most advanced).

   To these you also now recognize we should add:

3. They should be compatible with your own educational philosophies and lifelong aims for your child. (File Copy A)

4. They should reflect as much as possible your child's learning abilities, interests, needs and style. (Worksheet 3)

5. They should cover the subject areas you are required to teach and those you have elected to teach. (File Copy B)

You will be able to begin your list of subject area goals and objectives, subject-by-subject, yourself. It is logical, for example, that learning colors is basic to a beginning art education and that learning numbers is basic to a beginning math education. Were your child a kindergarten or first grade level student, you could come up with goals and objectives related to colors and numbers yourself. You would logically surmise that these basic elements of art and math should be included.

However, eventually you may want to check your roster of goals and objectives for items you may have overlooked or that may be less familiar to you. Or perhaps an entire subject area is unfamiliar to you, and thus you need help from a source other than yourself. In these cases, to locate typical age/grade appropriate goals and objectives, you can look to several sources:

1. Your sample curriculums (borrowed from other home-school parents, a local school, your state department of education, or a college library).

2. Sample grade level textbooks (borrowed from other parents, teachers, a school principal or superintendent, or a college library). Textbook teacher's editions may also be useful, particularly when they include a scope and sequence chart and/or cumulative progress chart, either of which could provide a hierarchy of curriculum goals for the subject treated in the textbook.

3. An experienced home, public, or private school teacher of the subject who is familiar with typical curricula for your child's grade level in that subject.

4. An expert in the field of study which puzzles you — someone who could help you arrive at a sequential set of learning steps in that subject/field.

5. Books written by experts about how to teach a particular subject/field. Check libraries or bookstores for these. (Also see resource lists beginning on p. 149 in this book.)

6. The "K-6 Subject Area Breakdown" on pages 91-148, which provides a typical grade-by-grade breakdown for each subject area noted in Chapter Three. This breakdown doesn't actually give you goals and objectives, but helps you realize categories for which you might write goals and objectives.

But first, let's rely on you. Using your File Copy B "My Child's Home-School Subjects," determine the number of subjects you have listed That number tells you how many sheets of fresh paper you now need in order to begin writing the curriculum in rough form for each subject, or how many copies to make of Worksheet 5, "Rough Copy Curriculum Sheet," on page 49. Six subjects? Six sheets. Seven subjects? Seven sheets. At the top of each sheet, write the name of one subject.

Now select the subject you feel you are most familiar with, and begin to think about the most basic skills and knowledge a person would need in order to begin learning about that subject. If your child is a beginner, perhaps at the kindergarten/first/second grade level, you may not need to go much beyond the basic skills and knowledge. If your child is more advanced, continue thinking. What skills and knowledge go beyond the basics? Think in a sequential fashion, from the most basic skills and knowledge on up to the more advanced. Consult one or more of the above six sample sources as needed.

At the same time, consider your child's present abilities and needs in that subject. Where is your child with respect to that subject now? At what level of proficiency? What skills and knowledge does she already have? What would/should be her next step towards greater proficiency? It is at that step that you are likely to begin her present curriculum — you would begin at her present ability level. Think, too, of any weak skills or needs for review and practice that she has demonstrated in that subject area. Perhaps her current learning goals in that subject should backtrack a bit to enable review and extra practice. If so, backtrack.

Worksheet 5
Rough Copy Curriculum Sheet

Subject: _____

Goals	Objectives
The student will be able to:	The student will be able to:
1.	1.1.
	1.2.
	1.3.
	1.4
2.	2.1.
	2.2.
	2.3
	2.4
3.	3.1
	3.2
	3.3
	3.4
4.	4.1
	4.2
	4.3
	4.4
5.	5.1
	5.2
	5.3
	5.4

Use photocopy master.

Let's look at an example. If we were considering a reading curriculum for a six-year-old, first-grade level student, we would think sequentially of some of the phonics (letter-sound association) elements of beginning reading:

The student will be able to...

1. identify upper and lower case alphabet letters at random

2. recognize the connection between letters and words on a page and the words that are read aloud by an adult

3. use the sound/sounds associated with beginning consonant letters, vowels, consonant combinations (such as, cl, st, ch, sh, ck), and vowel combinations (such as, ee, ea, ia, ou) to decode single-syllable words

4. use letter-sound associations to decode suffixes (word endings, such as -ing, -ly, -ness) and prefixes (word beginnings, such as, un-, pre-, and re-)

5. recognize root words in words that have suffixes and prefixes

6. recognize that a compound word can be formed by the joining of two words

...and so on.

Let's imagine that you have already taught the alphabet to our hypothetical six-year-old, and that she can put the letters in order and identify each upper and lower case letter by name at random (objective 1 above). Let's further imagine that you've read lots of stories to her and in the process pointed out words as you read, so that you feel she realizes that the symbols (letters) on the page represent the sounds you make when you read the page (objective 2). In other words, she understands the link between spoken and written words.

What she doesn't know, however, is that a certain single letter or combination of two or three letters represents a certain single or blended sound (objective 3). This tells us that her ability level is objective 2, and that she is ready for the next skill level or objective 3, and that she should in a year's time be able to move through several of the following objectives. So we would begin her written curriculum with objective 3 (calling it "1" in her current curriculum, of course). The general goal for the year, with respect to the decoding or phonics aspect of reading may be that *the student will be able to decode (figure out or read) one-and two-syllable words*. Each objective, beginning with the third objective above, would lead towards that goal. This segment of the curriculum, then, would look like this:

Subject: **READING**

Goals	Objectives
The student will be able to:	The student will be able to:
1. decode one- and two-syllable words	1.1 use the sound/sounds associated with beginning consonant letters, vowels, consonant combinations and vowel combinations to decode single-syllable words
	1.2 use letter-sound associations to decode suffixes and prefixes
	1.3 recognize root words in words that have suffixes and prefixes
	1.4 recognize that a compound word can be formed by the joining of two words

Would this segment pass the test of a good curriculum? Let's see.

THE TEST OF A GOOD HOME-SCHOOL CURRICULUM

1. Is this curriculum segment consistent with my educational philosophies? Can I infuse it with my philosophies to whatever extent I wish as I teach?

2. Does this curriculum segment fit into the lifelong aims of my child's education? Does this segment in the long run lead towards educated adulthood, as I have defined it?

3. Does it begin at my child's ability level and allow me to teach to my child's learning needs?

4. When I design lessons covering this segment of my child's curriculum, will I be free to include activities and methods that allow for my child's learning interests and learning style?

5. Is it age/grade appropriate for my child?

6. If objectives are included, are they sequential; that is, arranged from the most basic learning steps to the more advanced?

7. Are the goals and the objectives stated in terms of what the child will demonstrate s/he knows or can do?

If the answers to these seven questions are "yes," then you would probably consider the above or any "tested" curriculum segment satisfactory. It would become one part of your home-school year's reading curriculum.

Now, what about the other parts of your reading curriculum? Or the parts of curriculums for other subjects you might teach. On pages 40-42 we looked at rosters of subjects or courses typically taught at the primary, intermediate/junior high, and high school levels. Now we're ready to break each subject down further, to determine more specifically what areas of each subject are likely to become grade-level goal statements in your curriculum. In other words *reading* may be the identified subject, and *phonics* the identified narrower subject category within reading instruction, but what are the likely goal areas within phonics? In the above curriculum segment, for instance, *decoding one- and two-syllable words* was the goal category.

On pp. 47-48, six sources of help were listed which will give you clues to the goal categories to include. One of the six was the "K-6 Subject Area Breakdown." This breakdown, which appears on pages 91-148, is not a curriculum *per se*, but rather a list of categories upon which a curriculum could be based. Please remember as you read the breakdown that the list is typical and therefore generally acceptable. It contains no deliberate reflection of anyone's philosophies or lifelong learning goals for children. It is simply an unbiased, unslanted, impartial list of learning categories within each subject. Use it as a guide, not as a mandate. Let it help you decide which goal categories you want to include so that your curriculum is well-rounded, and then while actually writing your curriculum, slant the goals and objectives statements to whatever philosophical bent you wish.

As you read the subject breakdowns, keep in mind the grade-levels. Realize, for example, that at the lower levels subject coverages are basic and sometimes broad, informal or explorative. Also please realize that with such subjects as science and social studies, the focus is narrow — close to home — with the younger children, and then gradually widens as the child grows older and expands his knowledge and experience base. In addition, at any level the introductory stages of a sequence of lessons may be limited to *awareness* or *exploration*. Methods of teaching are up to you. Each subject, goal, and objective you include in your curriculum may be taught through any variety of activities, for your child and you are fully free to set the pace and tone of your daily lessons.

Your task now, then, is to locate your child's subjects in the breakdown and to select items you feel are appropriate for his curriculum. Then begin to roughly write out on your six (or seven or more) sheets of paper the goals and objectives you think are suitable for your child's curriculum. Use the examples of goals and objectives given earlier in this chapter and your sample curriculums as a guide to how to state your goals and objectives. Feel free to let your philosophies and aims (File Copy A) influence the tone of your goals and objectives. Also keep Worksheet 3 close at hand so it may lend direction to your thinking as you plan goals and objectives that suit your child's learning abilities, needs, interests, and style. This may, in fact, be an excellent time to involve your child in your curriculum-writing process.

When you have completed your rough curriculum, you will have the most time consuming and most difficult of your tasks done. The meat of your child's curriculum will have been formed. You'll be ready then to refine your rough work. So when you have completed your rosters of goals and objectives on separate pieces of paper, one copy of Worksheet 5 for each subject, take those sheets of paper, along with File Copies A and B and Worksheet 3, with you to Chapter Five, "Refining Your Rough Curriculum."

5

REFINING YOUR ROUGH CURRICULUM
A Touch of Polish

You now have a curriculum — *your* curriculum for *your* child. However, we do need to refine it — spruce it up, if you will, and make doubly sure it reflects your philosophies and the lifelong aims of your child's education, as well as suits your child's learning abilities, interests, needs, and style.

So on a large tabletop, spread out your two file copies, A and B, your Worksheet 3, and the batch of Worksheet 5's on which you have written your rough curriculum. **Beginning with File Copy B, "My Child's Home-School Subjects," do a quick cross check to make sure you've included each of your required and selected subjects on your rough copy curriculum sheets.** Then set File Copy B aside.

Second, do a cross check with File Copy A, "My Educational Philosophies and the Lifelong Aims of My Child's Education." This check should be more deliberate because you'll want to look at your rough goals and objectives from two angles:

1. Are all subject area learning goals and objectives consistent with your philosophies and lifelong educational aims for your child?

2. Where can you revise your subject area learning goals and objectives statements so they better reflect your philosophies and the lifelong aims of your child's education?

While not every goal and objective needs to reflect your philosophies and lifelong aims, there are likely to be several which you have stated in an unbiased manner but which could/should couch a philosophical slant. For example, an objective which states "The student will be able to cut basic figures with scissors." really doesn't need to mirror a philosophical angle. Further, if cutting figures with scissors is a basic step in a lifelong aim involving appreciation of fine arts, then again it need not be refined. However, you may want to include a philosophical slant somewhere in your child's art curriculum. Perhaps environmental issues are included in your educational philosophies. In that case you may want to emphasize designs, textures, and colors in nature; animal "artists;" natural beauty; symmetry and asymmetry in nature; the hidden beauty in ugly creatures;

landscape art; flower art, natural clays and glazes, and pottery-making — in other words, your art goals and objectives may couch the basics of environmental awareness and sensitivity.

Beginning reading goals and objectives may likewise vary in focus with regards to your philosophies and aims. Let's imagine, for instance, one of your lifelong aims for your child involves his playing an active role in community affairs. Phonics goals and objectives are likely to remain unslanted — focusing on the skills themselves. But when literature is covered, your goals and objectives may be infused with your philosophical focus. Perhaps you'll write objectives, for example, that emphasize biographies of people who have affected their communities in positive ways, stories involving community life in which leadership is a key factor, and nonfiction which includes various community elements — city governments, residential sections, community events, charitable groups, volunteerism, and so on. (This doesn't mean nothing else can be read. Other goals and objectives involving other kinds of literature may also be included.)

Perhaps Christianity is a key factor in your philosophies and lifelong aims for your child. You can easily instill many subject area goals and objectives with a Christian focus. Art objectives may include an appreciation of great Christian art, Bible illustration, and major Christian artists. Literature objectives may, of course, include Bible stories written for your child's level, the Bible as literature, Christian poetry, and so on. Biblical history may be the foundation of your history curriculum, and creation science the baseline of your science curriculum. It is possible to weave aspects of Christian life and learning into virtually every subject area.

Realize, too, that even if many of your written goals and objectives do not reflect your philosophies and lifelong aims for your child, you will be totally free to create daily lessons that do. So while you'll want to try to integrate your philosophies and lifelong aims into your rough, written curriculum, don't fret that you'll miss a chance to do so somewhere. Your curriculum is not a set of shackles; it won't restrict you, indeed can't restrict you, from being lavishly influenced by your philosophies and lifelong aims day-to-day as you teach your child — no matter how closely you follow your curriculum in your daily lessons.

So, carefully read each of your learning goals and objectives in each subject area to make sure they are consistent with your philosophies, and refine those that could be and/or should be philosophically slanted or slanted more towards a lifelong aim you hold for your child. Then set File Copy A aside.

Third, using Worksheet 3, "My Child," scan each goal and objective again to refine those that could be more in tune with your child's academic interests and abilities, special learning needs, and his learning style.

Have you blended his interests and abilities into the goals and objectives wherever possible to insure that his curriculum will be a challenge, a fascination, and a pleasure? If he loves music and plays a musical instrument, for example, have you worked music even into his math curriculum? Counting notes, beats, measures; noting musical sound patterns; analyzing the numerical combinations of instruments included in an orchestra, and so on? Do his history goals and objectives allow the two of you, teacher and student, to explore ways in which the fine arts mirror societal trends? Will his science lessons touch upon the dynamics of acoustics, decibels of musical sounds, physiological responses to music (e.g.: the calming effects of soothing music), and other such music-related science? Do his literature goals and objectives include biographies of musicians and composers?

If your child has special learning needs, they have likely been foremost in your mind, but check once again. Are there any goals and objectives which need to be modified to allow for your child's special needs? If, for instance, she is wheelchair bound, does your physical education curriculum include upper body exercises to the extent that she can perform them? Does it include physical therapy if called for by her condition? Does your science curriculum include the dynamics of motion, as it pertains to the wheelchair experience, and also as it pertains to those elements of motion she can not experience in her wheelchair? Do your reading goals and objectives allow for stories about very able disabled people? Will your history lessons bring out the role handicapped people have played in history — Franklin Roosevelt, for instance?

Remember that if your child has been identified as either physically or mentally handicapped on school records, it may be imperative in your state that you adapt your curriculum to meet her needs as a handicapped child. Nothing could leave you more open to child neglect charges than your ignoring such on-the-record special needs. In some cases, outside assistance will be warranted. If your child does need physical therapy, for example, does your curriculum allow for the services of a trained physical therapist? It should. If your child is hearing impaired, is she getting training pertinent to that handicap from a qualified adult? She should be. If your child has been identified as mentally retarded or learning disabled, how well does your curriculum meet her special learning needs? Is the help of a trained special education teacher advisable? If so, allow for that help in some of your goals and objectives. You needn't make elaborate statements about such assistance in your curriculum, but you should make sure your curricular goals and objectives address any special needs of your child, and you should note any assistance that is going to be provided to you or your child by special education personnel.

If your child has been identified on-the-record as "gifted or talented," you needn't be concerned with acquiring the assistance of another adult necessarily, but your goals and objectives should demonstrate that *you* will teach to your child's special giftedness and/or talent. If, for example, your child has been identified as gifted in math, you may include goals and objectives which allow for advanced math, computer applications of math, math exploration and invention, practical application of math (such as using math in bookkeeping for a small business), attendance at math-related youth camps and conferences, even perhaps working with a math mentor for a period of time. In other words, your child's math curriculum will show that you intend to take your gifted child beyond what is typically presented as math lessons to students of your child's age/grade.

Next, use Worksheet 3 to recheck how well your rough curriculum allows for your child's learning style. You will undoubtedly do more in daily lessons that leans towards his learning style than is indicated in his curriculum. Nevertheless, check your rough curriculum to make sure you haven't emphasized learning through your child's least adept modes of learning and that you have allowed for learning through his best modes. If he is highly verbal/sound oriented, for example, make sure his goals and objectives are infused with lots of opportunities for listening and talking, discussion, questioning and answering, interviewing, reciting, singing, and so on. If he is sensory oriented, for another example, ensure that his goals and objectives involve exploration and hands-on manipulation. If needed, integrate more of these kinds of opportunities into your goals and objectives statements. Then set Worksheet 3 aside.

Finally now, look back at "The Test of a Good Home-school Curriculum" on page 51. We've covered each item in the test, but just for one last check, go through the test to see if your curriculum "passes." Are there any final adjustments or refinements you still want to make in the wording of your Worksheet 5 rough goals and objectives? Do you need to consult with your child regarding any alterations?

Then, let's look at the overall form and appearance of your curriculum. At this point it is rough. You'll need to make a clean copy and, if it might ever be submitted to officials, make it *look* polished or official. We will also need to add a final item: a texts and materials list. When finished, in polished form, your curriculum will include four segments:

1. **A cover sheet.**

2. **A page based upon File Copy A and File Copy B. This page will contain a statement/paragraph identifying your educational philosophies, a roster of the lifelong learning aims you hold for your child, and a list of the subjects you have included in your curriculum.**

3. **Several pages containing your subject area goals and objectives. (based on copies of Worksheet 5)**

4. **A page listing texts and materials you plan to use as you teach your curriculum. (Worksheet 6)**

Let's concern ourselves with polishing segments 1, 2 and 3 in this chapter, and then we'll add segment 4 in the next chapter.

Segment 1, the cover sheet, should be a page which gives your document a title. You should also note towards the bottom of the sheet your child's age, address, and teacher's name (you).

If you want an official-looking document, the cover sheet, and all the other pages of your curriculum, should be typed or computer printed on nice quality, white, 8 1/2 x 11-inch paper. If you can't type or print it, perhaps you have a friend who would type it free of charge, or perhaps you could hire a typist — at an expense far below that of a purchased curriculum. Watch carefully for mechanical errors — spelling, grammar, and punctuation. You'll want each page of your curriculum to exhibit your own competence as a person and home teacher. Make it speak well of you! Mechanical perfection and the overall unblemished appearance of your curriculum, page-after-page, are important reflections of you.

Here's a small-sized version of a curriculum cover sheet.

Curriculum Sample: Cover Sheet

Grade Two
Home-School Curriculum
for Dancy Stone

Age: 7

Address: 111 Landslide Street
           Talus Slope KS 22222

Home Teacher: Merry Stone, mother

Having completed your cover sheet, Segment 1 is done, and you're ready to write Segment 2 in finished form. Look to File Copy A and File Copy B to complete Segment 2, which will become page 2 in your curriculum.

As a first entry below the title, type "My Educational Philosophies," or to include you and your spouse, "Our Educational Philosophies." Then copy your paragraph from File Copy A titled "Statement of My Educational Philosophies." Below that, type "The Lifelong Educational Aims of _____'s Schooling." Then copy your list of lifelong aims from File Copy B. Finally, type "_____'s Home-School Subjects." Refer to File Copy B to type a list of the subjects you have included in your child's curriculum. That's it! Segment 2 is completed.

Curriculum Sample: Philosophies, Aims, Subjects Sheet

PHILOSOPHIES, AIMS, SUBJECTS

My (Our) Educational Philosophies:

The Lifelong Educational Aims of Dancy Stone's Schooling:

1.
2.
3.
4.
5.
6.
7.

Dancy Stone's Home-School Subjects:

1.
2.
3.
4.
5.
6.
7.

You need now to revise and polish your Worksheet 5 rough copy curriculum sheets. One-by-one, type each set of subject area learning goals and objectives on fresh sheets of paper. Be sure to heed all the corrections, revisions, and refinements you've noted. Below is a sampling of what a couple of these curriculum pages might look like.

Curriculum Sample: Goals and Objectives

<u>GRADE 2</u>   <u>Subject: MATH</u>

GOALS: The student will be able to:

OBJECTIVES: The student will be able to:

1. recognize and work with the number words and number symbols from 1-100

1.1. read, write, compare, and order the number symbols from 1-100

1.2. read, write, compare, and order the number words from 1-100

1.3. identify groups of objects by number words and symbols 1-100

1.4. match number symbols with number words 1-100

1.5. recognize orally the ordinal numbers 1-20 (e.g. first, second, third, fourth, etc.)

1.6. use the ordinal numbers to place items in order

1.7. understand "odd" and "even" with respect to numbers

2. complete basic computations in addition and subtraction

2.1. recall basic addition and subtraction facts from memory

2.2. add two single digit numbers and add two double digit numbers

2.3. mentally add multiples of tens and multiples of hundreds

2.4. estimate mentally the sums of two numbers

2.5 use addition and subtraction to solve simple, practical math-related problems

<u>GRADE 2</u>   Subject: <u>SCIENCE</u>

GOALS: The student will   OBJECTIVES: The student will be
        be able to: able to:

1. recognize and describe   1.1. identify, describe, and illustrate
   elements of climate   the four seasons

                                1.2. name several kinds of weather
                                     and recognize that weather is
                                     constantly changing

                                1.3. explain causes of common
                                     weather changes (e.g. clouds
                                     bring rain, sun increases
                                     warmth, cold turns rain to
                                     snow, etc.)

                                1.4. recognize that climates vary
                                     from place to place

2. recognize the pervasive-   2.1. recognize that much of the earth
   ness and qualities of   is composed of rocks and cov-
   rocks and water on the   ered by water
   earth
                                2.2. describe basic properties of
                                     rocks

                                2.3. identify and differentiate among
                                     sand, pebble, rock or stone,
                                     boulder, mountain

                                2.4. describe basic properties of
                                     water

                                2.5. explain the visible effects of
                                     weather on water (e.g., waves)

                                2.6. identify lake, stream, ocean

3. recognize the relation-   3.1. explain the positions of the sun,
   ship between the sun,   moon, and earth, using models
   moon, and earth
                                3.2. describe "orbit"

                                3.3. explain how/why the moon
                                     shines

                                3.4. recognize that the sun provides
                                     earth with both light and heat

4. recognize the difference   4.1. identify living and nonliving
between living and nonliv-   things
ing things
                                4.2. explain basic differences
                                     between living and nonliving
                                     things

                                4.3. recognize the great diversity of
                                     nonliving and of living things

...and so on. This is how the entire subject segment of your curriculum should look — a logical arrangement with grade level identified first, subject areas noted atop each subject section, goals numbered and listed on the left, each followed by numbered objectives listed on the right. Curriculums do not have to be arranged in this particular fashion, but this arrangement is standard, and thus a good one to use if format is important to you or to anyone who may review your curriculum. It is also a well-organized means of providing yourself with a complete and usable curriculum guide.

Whew! Your efforts with this chapter have been great. And you will be rewarded! In the mass-production system that public education is, your child would never glean the advantages that your home-written curriculum will allow. Even the use of commercial home curriculums could not fully provide the unique and personal characteristics of your own curriculum. Through your efforts, you will feel more confident than ever that your own concept of your child's education will be realized. And through your efforts, you will give your child an extraordinary gift: an education uniquely suited to him or her. In other words, your efforts will have been exceedingly well spent.

Upon completion of the typing of your subject area goals and objectives, you will have finished Segment 3 and will be ready to go on to our final segment, "Texts and Materials." Not all curriculums include a texts and materials list, but many do. Often such a list is required of home schoolers. Sometimes even teaching methods and learning activities are included. The actual writing of your "Texts and Materials" page will be easy, but looking for materials to correlate with your curriculum may not be so easy. Thus, the next chapter is devoted to this endeavor and to the writing of that simple Segment 4 page, "Texts and Materials."

As you turn to this next chapter, leave your file copies and your worksheets behind, but bring along your polished cover sheet, philosophies/aims/subjects page, and your subject area goals and objectives pages.

6

TEXTS AND MATERIALS

Appropriate Selection, Appropriate Use

Congratulations, you have just given yourself and your child a low-cost/no-cost curriculum for your upcoming home-school year! And it's a curriculum more suited for you and your child than any other curriculum could possibly be. Thinking about how you'll teach your curriculum is your next step. One element in deciding *how* is selecting textbooks and other teaching materials.

Where do you look for texts and materials? There are hundreds of text and materials catalogs available throughout the country — some particularly for home schools and others for any schools — and all listed in various home-school guides, such as the comprehensive HOME SCHOOL: TAKING THE FIRST STEP. A local home-school support group or a local school or church may make catalogs available. You can often find text and materials advertisements, lists, and product reviews in general or home-school parent magazines. However, while you'll no doubt eventually obtain several suppliers' catalogs, you may begin by looking closer to home. Closer-to-home sources of texts and materials are likely to be as low-cost/no-cost as the curriculum you have just given yourself.

Libraries often carry textbooks and other academic books and materials. College libraries, particularly those which serve students training to be teachers, almost always carry K-12 texts. Also, the local public schools may have storage copies of texts for all the courses they teach. These stored texts may be available to you, either through a local principal or a friendly teacher who will loan you a copy. Used-book bookstores, college bookstores which carry returned books on a "used" shelf, and sometimes even regular bookstores may be sources. Government agencies and civic or social organizations often offer free and/or inexpensive educational materials to home schoolers and others. Parent-teachers who have been home schooling a year or more may have old texts and materials which they may be happy to sell cheaply or loan to you. Some home-school support organizations maintain lenders' collections of texts and materials or host flea market sales of used books. If you're living in Alaska, check with your state department of education's correspondence course division for texts to use with their correspondence home courses. These books, if returned, are cost-free.

More important than the source of your texts and materials, however, is your selection of appropriate texts and materials. Now that you've gone to the trouble of writing your own curriculum for your child, you'll want to ensure that the texts and materials you select will enhance your lessons, not detract from or negate your curriculum. You'll want to ensure, too, if you use textbooks in daily lessons, that any curriculum inherent in a textbook series does not override your own curriculum. Textbooks can provide direction, background information, examples, activities, and serve as references, while not dominating, but instead supporting and complementing your curriculum. You'll want texts and materials that do what you want them to do, that will help you teach the way you want to teach, that will allow your child to learn at his level and in the way he wants to learn, and that are consistent with the philosophies and lifelong aims that you have carefully framed for your child's education.

So first look closely at each text's table of contents, the vocabulary, sentence style and length, the readability of the book's print, and the kinds of activities it includes or recommends. Make sure each text is well-suited for your child — considering his interests, abilities, needs, and learning style.

Read one chapter or unit to get an idea of the depth of the text's content coverage. With briefer, nontextual materials, you may be able to read the entire content. Do the materials provide the kind of coverage, reference information, and/or activities that you want? If the subject is unfamiliar to you, you may want a full text that covers the subject in depth. If the subject is familiar to you, you may decide a shallower content coverage is fine because you'll be able to fill in the gaps and may even like the idea of being free of the text for the most part. For example, if American literature is a subject you'll teach and for which you have much background, you'll be able to tell your child all about prominent writers, major periods in writing, styles of writing, the connections between literature and historical or social trends and events, and so on. For you, then, a collection of American literature will do. On the other hand, if American literature is not so familiar to you, you may want a comprehensive textbook or anthology which offers thorough background discussions for each group of literary pieces it includes.

Also, if the subject is unfamiliar to you, you may wish to secure a teacher's manual to accompany the text you choose. In many cases most of the recommended lesson activities will be explained only in the teacher's edition. Oftentimes a science textbook, for instance, will provide description, discussion, illustration, and questions for each area covered, while the accompanying teacher's manual will recommend experiments, field work, and other firsthand learning activities. If the latter activities interest you and your child most, you may find such a manual useful as a reference. Teachers' manuals may be secured from the same sources noted above for texts and materials. The manuals can be richly useful. You may even discover that a teacher's manual will suffice for any lesson activities in a familiar subject area, and that the accompanying student textbook is not needed at all.

Next, by reading a chapter or unit of the student text (or teacher's manual) and then scanning the rest of the book, you'll get a feel for the overall tone of the text — a reflection of the author's or authors' philosophies. Let your own stated philosophies and long-term aims function as a screening device for both text and materials companies and for the texts, materials, and teacher's manuals themselves. In other words, look to those companies whose materials generally appear compatible with your philosophies. If, for example, you want to anchor your child's curriculum in Christian principles, it may be beneficial to look first to those suppliers who offer primarily Christian texts and materials. If, in addition, one of your aims is that your child become an independent, analytical thinker, look to those texts and materials which allow much nontextual, explorative learning and that stimulate diverse, higher level thinking. By doing so you remain in control of the directions and focuses of your child's learning.

Don't rush. While it is possible to teach many lessons without textbooks and commercial materials, you may want to lean to some extent in at least some subjects on the information provided through good textbooks and other materials, even though your own curriculum will be your overriding guide. So look well to find those most appropriate and most useful for you and your child. Once you've spent your now saved curriculum dollars on a few textbooks and materials, you'll want to be able to use those texts and materials at least as references...and to not have wasted your money!

Keep running note sheets, Worksheet 6 on p. 69, of the texts and materials you review. Make copies of the worksheet — one copy for each subject you plan to teach. For each subject, jot down those texts and materials that appear appealing to you. Next note the supplier of those texts and materials — when you find out who supplies them. Jot down your reactions and thoughts as you peruse and evaluate each text or teaching material at which you look. Last, note anything you have heard or read about them that attracted you to them.Then select. Fill out File Copy C, p. 70, after you have made your selections for each subject.

Note the last line on File Copy C, " Our Basic Reference Library." Here you should list any dictionaries, thesauruses, grammar handbooks, atlas's, and encyclopedia sets that you will have on hand for use in all subject areas. Select these in the same careful manner as your texts and other materials. From grade one on, you should have at least one age/grade appropriate English language dictionary. From grade four on, you should have at least one atlas, one thesaurus, and one grammar handbook. (This is not to suggest that they couldn't also be useful earlier.) Encyclopedia sets are expensive and quickly outdated — you may elect to simply note the names and locations of those sets available for use by your children in a nearby public library, school library, home-school lenders' library, or even at a neighbor's house. Using File Copy C, you'll now be ready to type the last page of your curriculum, the "Texts and Materials" page.

As you type this final page of your curriculum, you can make it look much like File Copy C on p. 70 or alter it as you wish. Do make it look organized and remember to underline titles of textbooks and other books you list. Then attach it to the back of the rest of your curriculum, and you'll have —

1. one cover sheet

2. one philosophies/aims/subjects sheet

3. several subject area goals and objectives sheets

4. one text and materials sheet

And then, you're done! You have a wonderful, personalized (and FREE!) guide to your own home-school year with your child, and you have an official-looking curriculum to present to school officials (or a lawyer) if ever necessary.

You may at some time be in the position of having to prove that you've used your curriculum. The next chapter will show you ways in which you can document that your curriculum indeed has been a viable guide, that you have used it during your home-school year, and that your child has progressed through the sequence of goals and objectives outlined in your curriculum.

Worksheet 6
Texts and Materials Evaluation

Subject:_____

Text/Material Title	Supplier Address and Item's Price	My Evaluation
1.		
2.		
3.		
4.		
5.		

Make duplicate copies of this page – one for each subject.

Use photocopy master.

File Copy C

THE TEXTBOOKS AND MATERIALS
I WILL USE TO TEACH MY CHILD'S CURRICULUM

Subject:_____   Texts/Materials:

Subject:_____   Texts/Materials:

Subject:_____   Texts/Materials:

Subject:_____   Texts/Materials:

Subject:_____   Texts/Materials:

Subject:_____   Texts/Materials:

Subject:_____   Texts/Materials:

Subject:_____   Texts/Materials:

Subject:_____   Texts/Materials:

Subject:_____   Texts/Materials:

Subject:_____   Texts/Materials:

Our Basic Reference Library

_____   _____

_____   _____

_____   _____

Use photocopy master.

7

DOCUMENTING THE USE OF YOUR CURRICULUM
A Home-Ed Travel Log

You may want to make a duplicate copy of your entire curriculum, from cover sheet to text/materials sheet, and secure the original copy in a safe place away from your working copy. If you are required to submit your curriculum to school officials, give them the original copy after making *two* extra copies for yourself. One duplicate will be the aforementioned safe copy and the other your working copy. The former will remain secured in case something should happen to the working copy. The latter you'll use as your planning and teaching guide day-by-day.

In some states or school districts, school officials will review home-schoolers' files to verify that the curriculum is first of all on-hand and, second, is being or has been followed during the home-school year. If yours is such a state or district, this chapter is especially for you. If yours is not such a state or district, please consider whether it *may* be at some future time necessary for you to prove the use of your child's curriculum. Is an official review or litigation a likely or even remote possibility? If so, you may want to read this chapter and follow some of its recommendations. If not, you may nevertheless benefit by having for yourself accurate records of the goals and objectives you've covered, activities and materials you've included, ongoing projects that involve further followup, and records of your child's achievement. You and your child may also simply enjoy having a scrapbook, so to speak, or a "travel log" of your home-education journey, records that you may thumb through many times over the years.

Certain types of documents can be designed and maintained on a regular basis to demonstrate what your child has actually studied and, thereby, to verify that you have followed your curriculum. Among such documents are the following:

1. Subject area student portfolios

2. A lesson plan book

3. A teacher's daily log

4. Tests and other assessments

5. A grade book

6. A narrative

7. A cumulative permanent record

Let's take a look at each of these documents as potential means of verifying that you and your child have followed your curriculum. You won't need to develop all seven of these, but may select perhaps two or three to use as verification. Some may even be required in your state.

Subject area student portfolios are both easy and fun to keep and can provide a clear representation of what your child has studied. They are easy because you simply have to create a file for each subject and drop in completed assignments, projects, writings, drawings, etc., from time to time. You would select those items which seem most representative of what your child has studied — perhaps the final activity or project of each unit of study, for instance. For some subject areas, however, you may wish to keep all completed activities and projects — art projects, for example. Your portfolios can become delightful albums of your child's progress, albums she, you, siblings, grandfolks, and friends will have fun reminiscing over now and then.

Always date and keep portfolio papers in chronological order. This will allow not only a review of what your child has studied, but will demonstrate the order in which she has covered the sequential goals and objectives of her curriculum. In other words, this order will verify that you and she have followed the curriculum in sequence, from the least to the more advanced goals and objectives. A portfolio's chronological order will also reveal her academic progress. Her first-of-the-year work will show less proficiency and narrower focus than later projects. You, she, and any school officials who may look through her portfolios will quickly note that she is progressing.

A second kind of documentation widely used is a teacher's lesson plan book. In a lesson plan book the home teacher jots down her planned activities, textbook pages to be covered, learning tasks and projects to be completed, etc., for each week's upcoming lessons. She also notes materials, aids, real life settings, resource people, assessments, and such, which she plans to use with each lesson. Commercially made plan books are used routinely by public and private school teachers and are available to you at teacher supply stores which can be found in most large cities. You could also create your own in a 3-ring binder or borrow one page from a local school teacher and make enough copies for your home-school year. A lesson plan book contains enough weekly plan layouts for each week of the year. On each week's planning pages there are five horizontal rows, one for each day Monday through Friday, and several vertical columns, one for each subject. See Documentation Sample: "Lesson Plan Book" at the end of this chapter.

Planning lessons in a plan book requires some forethought. The teacher must set aside time near the end of each week to write out the next week's plan. However, despite the effort such plan-writing requires, many home teachers use lesson plans to remain organized, to prepare ahead of time for upcoming learning activities, and to ensure a sequential order to the lessons. Lesson planning is indeed a terrific means of remaining organized. Besides serving in these ways as an organizer and a guide for the home teacher, the written lesson plans serve as a permanent record of what the home-schooled child has studied — in other words, as proof that the child has followed her curriculum.

If you elect to not write lesson plans, you may want instead to keep a teacher's daily log. A log is much like a journal, but with a special purpose. To keep a log, at the end of each day you will sit down to record the day's learning activities, subject-by-subject. You may also include notations about the progress you have observed in your child's learning. To start a log, just buy a lined notebook and date each page as you go, or buy an already dated datebook or journal. Then see Documentation Sample: "Teacher's Daily Log" at the end of this chapter.

A fourth option for documenting the use of your curriculum is to give and keep regular tests and other assessments. Those assessments given orally or simply through observation of your child's performance would need to be recorded on paper in some fashion with their results. All tests, assessments, or oral assessment records would be filed in a portfolio-style file folder to be kept throughout your home-school year. You would, in fact, be wise to keep records of major assessment results year-by-year. Each test and assessment that you file should be dated and arranged with the others in chronological order. They will then serve to highlight your child's progress as she moves through her home-school year of studies. The content of each test and assessment, which should be apparent on the papers you file, will correlate with the content of her curriculum and thereby verify that her curriculum is being followed. You may wish to staple a test/assessment log sheet to the front of the file. On this sheet you could write in the date, subject area, specific elements of the subject that were tested, and a score or some other descriptor showing the results of the test/assessment. See Documentation Sample: "Test Assessment File Log" at the end of this chapter.

Lesson plans or a daily log would be a good complement to a grade book. With a grade book you will record, daily or weekly, in some fashion your child's progress in each subject. Because traditionally teachers merely record letter grades or percentiles for each assignment or test in the graph-like grade books, the books are relatively uninformative. Your grade book, however, may be designed by you — with a more detailed itemization of your child's progress to date. This would provide a more thorough record of how well your child is moving along through her home-school curriculum. Documentation Sample: "Traditional Grade Book," at the end of this chapter provides an example of the typical teacher's grade book — a grid which could simply be a collection of 3-hole punched, purchased graph paper kept in a 3-ring binder. Documentation Sample: "Optional Grade

Book" suggests a possible alternative to the traditional grade book. The optional book gives you a chance to include informative details regarding your child's progress. You may elect, of course, as noted above, to design your own grade book, one that is well organized and includes a consistent but alternative means of recording progress.

Another option for documenting the use of your child's curriculum is a narrative report. To write a narrative, you or a certified teacher would write about your child's learning activities and progress in each subject. You may highlight the actual goals and objectives found in your child's curriculum by underlining or italicizing them in your narrative report. A narrative should probably be written every six to nine weeks throughout the home-school year and a lengthier, more comprehensive report at year's end. See Documentation Sample: "Narrative Report."

Finally, you may elect to keep what the professionals call a "cumulative permanent record." At the completion of each semester or year of home schooling, a simple record is prepared showing the student's courses for the year with grades, pass/fail status, or other descriptors of achievement for each course. The student's total days present and absent are also recorded. These records are written in a file or on a sheet of paper which has room for twelve, or with kindergarten thirteen, such yearly records. Typically achievement test results, if available, are also recorded on the file. This then becomes the student's *permanent file,* an entire kindergarten-through-twelfth-grade record. See Documentation Sample: "Cumulative Permanent Record."

Incidentally, if your child has previously attended a public school, a Cumulative Permanent Record already exists for him. Legally you have a right to see and copy the record — if you can do so without removing it from the school. This record can provide you with an official model for your own Cumulative Permanent Record and also with your child's previous grades, attendance records, and achievement test results which you can then record on your own permanent record.

Because the Cumulative Permanent Record is written in only on a semester or yearly basis, this document should always be accompanied by one or more of the other kinds of aforementioned documents that you maintain. In fact, any of the possible documents that verify the use of your child's curriculum should be maintained in combination with one or two other documents. Try to keep at least one of the more comprehensive records (such as the portfolio, plan book, or daily log) and then also keep one or two of the sketchier records (such as tests/assessments, grade book, narrative, or permanent record).

When you have decided which records to keep, design them and begin to routinely, consistently maintain each. Avoid letting them lapse, as catching up with such documents can be difficult and aggravating. Use them as complements to your curriculum — remembering that their purpose is to prove the use of your curriculum throughout your child's home-school year, and/or to provide yourself with an accurate, informative and interesting record of the educational route you and your child have followed. You will have with your records and your home-written curriculum an exceptionally sound verification of your child's studies and progress.

Worth noting here, too, is the fact that commercial curriculum suppliers (which are not low-cost/no-cost) often include record-keeping as one of the services you buy along with a purchased curriculum. These record-keeping services typically consist of the cumulative permanent file alone (semester and yearly course lists with grades, plus achievement test scores). As this chapter has demonstrated, you can keep these records yourself — free. Sometimes you'll discover, too, that a local home school organization will maintain a low-cost/no-cost record-keeping service — or you can help them start one. However, if you feel you need the legal security of record-keeping under the wing of an umbrella school, you may wish to pay for a record-keeping service.

As a final note, do realize that should you elect to enroll or reenroll your child in a public school, your curriculum and records will demonstrate what your child has studied, the scope and sequence of his lessons, his achievement, and whether or not he is "at grade level." Still later, when your child applies to a college or for a job, his curriculum and records will give him the information he needs to verify his education. Even transcripts of courses studied could be drawn from his curriculum and records. This, incidentally, is a good reason to keep each year's curriculum and records through and beyond his twelfth grade year.

Also, as a sideline benefit, at year's end you'll be ready to easily create a new (or not-so-new) curriculum and to develop continued documentation of the use of that new curriculum. We'll discuss this sideline benefit in the next chapter.

Documentation Sample: Lesson Plan Book

	LESSON PLANS		
Student _____		Week of _____ 19__ – 19__	
	subject:	subject:	subject:
Monday			
Tuesday			
Wednesday			
Thursday			
Friday			

Documentation Sample: Teacher's Daily Log

Home Teacher's Log
School Year: 1990-91
Home Student: Billy Miller   Grade: one
Home Teacher: Mazie Miller

Sept. 1: Morning, phonics — beginning consonant sounds; reading — oral paragraphs in the form of a simple recipe for no-bake cookies which Billy followed as I read; literature — an oral reading of *Frederick* by Leo Lionni followed by discussion of the central character, a mouse; math — counting and measurement — as we made the cookies; social studies — continued work on Billy's cardboard model of a metropolis he calls "Megalapatropolis. During lunch, science — watched a video documentary on African wildlife which Billy later discussed with his dad. Afternoon, litera- ture, science, & socialization — we joined other home schoolers for a trip to the library for the monthly Storybook Puppet Show, fol- lowed by a walk through the park to find leaf samples and to play with the other kids. Later, art, literature — Billy did a painting of a giraffe on the African plains and the usual bedtime story — this time *The Grey Lady and the Strawberry Snatcher* by Molly Bang.

Sept. 2: Morning, phonics — review and on to new consonants; reading — a letter from Billy's Aunt Goldie after which Billy reiter- ated to me the main things about which Aunt Goldie had written; writing — Billy dictated a letter to Aunt Goldie which I typed and read back to him and then he attempted with some success his own reading of the letter; art & science — Billy made a crayon stencil of three of the leaves he'd found in the park yesterday and then dictated to me brief paragraphs describing each leaf and the tree from which each came; math — counting the leaves he'd gath- ered and gluing them to a sheet of paper in order of size, smallest to largest, and discussing the comparative sizes of the trees from which the leaves had come. Afternoon, literature — *On Market Street* by Arnold Lobel, followed by Billy's oral story of what he'd do during a day on Market Street; music — piano lesson; physical education — fast-walking with his sister and the planning of what they called "A Super Health Nut Backyard Picnic Supper."

Sept. 3: Morning, math — counted people lining up for our home-schoolers' field trip bus ride and compared the number of children with the number of grown-ups, the number of boys with the number of girls, and the number of bus seats with the number of people; social studies — discussed with other home schooled children and their parents the many transportation systems avail- able in the U.S. and their advantages and disadvantages; science — visit to the Kansas City Nature Museum. Evening, literature — read *Ferdinand*, Billy's current favorite children's book.

Documentation Sample:
Test/Assessment File Log

Subject _____

	Date	Skills/Knowledge Area Tested	Results
1.	_____	_____	_____
2.	_____	_____	_____
3.	_____	_____	_____
4.	_____	_____	_____
5.	_____	_____	_____
6.	_____	_____	_____
7.	_____	_____	_____
8.	_____	_____	_____
9.	_____	_____	_____
10.	_____	_____	_____
11.	_____	_____	_____
12.	_____	_____	_____
13.	_____	_____	_____
14.	_____	_____	_____
15.	_____	_____	_____

DOCUMENTATION SAMPLE: TRADITIONAL GRADE BOOK

School _____   Teacher _____
School year _____   Semester ____   Quarter ____
Course/Subject _____

dates

students		M	T	W	T	F	M	T	W	T	F	M	T	
1. Mary Miller														
2. Susie Miller														
3. Tom Miller														

DOCUMENTATION SAMPLE: OPTIONAL GRADE BOOK

Record of Progress

Student _____   School Year_____
Course/Subject _____

	Date	Grade or Descriptor	Additional Comments
1.	____	_____	_____
2.	____	_____	_____
3.	____	_____	_____
4.	____	_____	_____
5.	____	_____	_____
6.	____	_____	_____

DOCUMENTATION SAMPLE: NARRATIVE REPORT

Annual Evaluation Narrative

Home Student: Billy Miller   Grade: one

Please note: The subject areas of Billy's studies appear in capital letters below and the specific learning objectives are underlined.

With respect to CHILDREN'S LITERATURE, Billy has logged a total of 144 children's books, including 19 Caldecott Award Books and other selections of children's literature, in his self-illustrated "Books I Have Listened To" scrapbook. He has spent no less than 30 minutes each home-school day listening to complete stories and to books of children's poetry.

Having enjoyed hundreds of poems by a wide variety of poets, including young poets featured in the children's magazine *Stone Soup,* Billy has developed a roster of his favorite poems and poets which he names and discusses with anyone interested and he can identify poetry by both its visual configuration in magazines and books and by its aural cadences when he hears it aloud.

He is also happy to pull out stories by his favorite authors and children's book illustrators whenever friends visit after school or on weekends. Prior to his "reading" of the book to a friend, he will identify the story characters and offer an overview of the events in the story. At times, he and a friend will abandon the books in our 60-volume library and simply tell stories of their own and now and then even create skits to depict their stories and present them to any available adults.

Billy has developed a great love for books during his first years of storybook experiences. Certain books have even become his "teddy bears" for bedtime sharing and cuddling. And his favorite building in Sky, Kansas, is the Sky Public Library. At the library he has also enjoyed the monthly Storybook Puppet Shows put on by the local arts association.

[Note: This portion would be only one segment of a larger evaluation narrative which would refer to all areas of the curriculum. By relying on your curriculum outline and your records of daily lessons, you should quickly and easily come up with the needed information.]

DOCUMENTATION SAMPLE: CUMULATIVE PERMANENT RECORD

Cumulative Record

School _____

Student's full name _____ Birthdate _____

Father's name _____

Mother's name _____

Parents' address_____

_____

Elementary

spelling	reading	math	science	soc st	music	art	health				absent	present	gr level	teacher

[Subjects may vary; use blank columns to add others.
Final grades are recorded on the grid for each subject area.]

**Junior High
High School**

[Grids similar to the one on the right are used to record each year's academic work for grades 7-12]

		Grade ___			
	course	sem 1	sem II	final grade	teacher
1.					
2.					
3.					
4.					
5.					
6.					

8

TRANSLATING YOUR CURRICULUM INTO LESSONS
Remaining in Control

You may be delighted now to have not just a home curriculum, but a low-cost/no-cost home-written home curriculum. Yet you may be wondering how you will use this curriculum to create daily lessons for your child. You may additionally want to know more about how to integrate your curricular areas, and how to work socialization into your lessons even though socialization is not a subject area in your curriculum. You may further wonder how you can let your child learn as a self-directed learner, if that is your bent, or through teacher-directed but unstructured lessons even though your written curriculum is structured.

To begin a discussion of these issues, we should clarify one important point. As an outcome of your work with this book, you will have written a structured curriculum, based upon your own and your child's desires and needs, yet officially apt. However, the important point to remember now is that your written curriculum, while itself structured, should be used flexibly. Everyday lessons, while rooted in your curriculum, may many times sway and veer in directions of their own. Let this swaying and veering happen...to an extent that still allows you to meet your self-selected goals for your child's education. No school official will be on hand to watch how strictly each lesson adheres to your curriculum. As stated earlier, you do want to develop a paper trail which documents that you have followed your curriculum, but this does not mean you must feel locked in, goal-by-goal and objective-by-objective, day-by-day. Your curriculum should provide you with a solid, useable daily/weekly *guide*; enabling you to offer your child a complete, sequential education; but it should not control you. You wrote it; you controlled its content, and now you should control its application. Thus think *flexible* when you create daily/weekly lessons.

With this basic understanding in mind, we can address the first issue raised above: how to translate your curricular goals and objectives into lessons. Lessons require some kind of planning — mental or written or both. Some home schoolers resist writing lesson plans and some are downright opposed to them, primarily because lesson plans are viewed as too confining or too structured. However, the *flexible* mindset is applicable to lesson plans as well as to curricula. Also, if you're not going to write out lesson plans, you can benefit from thinking about upcoming lessons in lesson-plan format, and therefore, from understanding the process of lesson planning. Indeed, many home schoolers rely heavily (and happily) on written lesson plans. The choice, of course, remains yours. For the sake of clarity in our discussion here, then, let's presume you'll write lesson plans.

To write your first week's lesson plans, you would look to the first goal or, in some cases, the first few goals of each subject area you plan to delve into during the first week. One subject at a time, jot down the essence of the first goal(s) and then consider how you will teach or help your child learn that goal. In other words, just brain-storm a bit, in general terms, about methods, settings, materials, and other resources for teaching to that goal. Enlist your youngster's help! Then look at the specific objectives you have listed which lead to the achievement of that goal. Since the objectives are in sequential order, begin, of course, with the first objective. How will you teach that objective? What textbooks, workbooks, reference books, and other materials will be needed? What activities will your child complete? What projects? What equipment should you have on hand? What settings will be appropriate, particularly for any hands-on or explorative activities? What other people might be involved? What will their roles be? What will your role be as your child works towards achieving this first objective? What will your child's role be? How many daily sessions might be needed for your child to achieve this objective? Will your child be working on more than one objective and/or goal at a time in a given subject area? Let's look at an example of how you might use the answers to questions like these.

Let's imagine that you are considering your child's Grade Two Science Curriculum (as in the example on p. 62). In your science curriculum several goals could be addressed simultaneously, but for now let's just address the first one: *The student will be able to recognize and describe elements of climate.* Upon first considering that goal and brainstorming a bit about how to teach to that goal, you may have thought of explorative learning in outdoor settings, of monitoring an outdoor thermometer, of terminology that may be important, of a visit to a local weather station, of trips to other climates/locales that you and your child have taken or could take, children's books that focus on climate, etc. Then you look at the first objective: *The student will be able to identify, describe, and illustrate the four seasons.* In your plan book you jot down the essence of the objective: "to identify, describe, illustrate the four seasons." "Let's see," you say to yourself, "this objective includes three things: identifying the four seasons, describing the four seasons, and illustrating the four seasons." "Hmmmm," you continue, "perhaps the identification aspect could best be approached in the field — outdoor exploration, and perhaps by remembering other climates/seasons we've experienced. Each evening, or during reading/literature time, we could read and discuss a children's book in which seasons are a key element. These books and maybe a visit to a weather station could help us identify seasons and also discover how other people describe the seasons. Then it will be time to find out if my child can describe the seasons herself. And then, can she illustrate each of the four seasons? Hmmmm," you conclude, "looks like a few days of lessons will be required."

And so on. So far on your lesson plan page, you have just jotted down the essence of the objective. Now decide which learning activities should occur first and be jotted down in your first day's lesson plan.

Perhaps for your first day you'll write: *Field trip from the warm river valley to chilly Saddle Mountain where autumn is already a season. We'll explore signs of the changing season.*

For your second day's plan, perhaps you'll write: *We'll discuss the signs of the autumn season we discovered yesterday and read the book Autumn is Here.*

For day three, perhaps you'll write: *We'll walk into the meadow to find still-blooming wildflowers and discuss what happened to earlier flowers, how long the current flowers will last, and why they will disappear. Also discuss the turning of the leaves and what color they used to be and what will happen to them next, and when they will return.*

For day four, perhaps you'll write: *We'll make crayon rubbings of a leaf — one green, one colored, one brownish-black, and one green again — to depict summer, autumn, the decaying leaves of winter, and spring. We'll also read The Four Seasons.*

For day five, perhaps you'll write: *We'll go out to watch the squirrels and chipmunks, to observe seasonal animal behavior. Then we'll read "Animals and the Seasons" in the science textbook.*

And with that you will have your first week's science lessons planned. (See the plan book sample on p. 76.) You will need to do a little mental work each day, too, in order to be sure you're prepared for each lesson. Do you need to arrange, for example, to have the car for the first day's field trip? Will a visit to the local library be necessary to secure copies of *Autumn is Here* and *The Four Seasons*? Will you need to walk to the meadow alone ahead of time to locate wildflowers for day three's lesson? For day four, do you have crayons and paper available? In other words, while you have successfully translated your curricular goal(s) and objective(s) into daily lesson plans, the plans will act as a guide, a prompt, if you will, to those preparations you need to complete in order to be fully ready to carry out your plans... and, thus, to teach your curriculum.

The second issue raised in the opening paragraph of this chapter regarded what is called the "integrated curriculum." In an integrated curriculum, subject areas spill over into one another. Writing, for example, may be taught/practiced in all subject areas, as well as during creative writing lessons. Likewise reading comprehension may be continually taught throughout most of each day's lessons. Science objectives may be developed during literature lessons. Social studies objectives may be woven into art objectives. Music objectives may be integrated into math objectives. In other words, elements of one subject may be indirectly taught during instruction of another subject. Why? In the "real" world, subject areas are not exclusive of each other. They are in dozens of ways related. Historical events and trends, for example, exert tremendous influence upon art and literature. Scientific research uncovers hundreds of examples of natural music. Math is essential to effective consumerism. Awareness of health concepts influences everyday home economics practices. In theory, then, if in real life what we call subject areas are interwoven in a multitude of ways, shouldn't they also be interwoven in our children's education? Proponents of the integrated curriculum respond with a resounding "yes" to this question, and educational research backs up their inclination to integrate their curriculums...and your inclination to integrate your curriculum.

You can accomplish an integrated curriculum by integrating objectives related to one subject area into another subject area, in the manner suggested above — science into music, history into art and literature, health into home economics, and so on. You can further integrate your curriculum through your daily lessons by making a conscious effort to not treat each subject in isolation. Instead, you may design lesson activities that focus on subject specific learning objectives, but which involve the practice and application of elements of other subjects, as suggested above, when possible and logical.

Related to the integrated curriculum concept is the third issue raised above: how to work socialization into your curriculum and lessons, even though socialization is not a subject area. Socialization can occur in a multitude of instances in conjunction with learning activities in any subject area. Your curricular goals and objectives may actually include mention of activities carried out with other family members, neighbors, other home-school youngsters, and involve various resource persons, experts, or practitioners. However, whether or not your goals and objectives statements mention educational socialization activities, those statements may be translated into lessons which do include other people.

In fact, by using your curriculum to design lessons that frequently include other people you can develop a *learning community* for your child — an elder who share-teaches a craft with your child, community service folks who involve your child in their work, neighbors with whom he can exchange learning opportunities, group experiences with other children and adults, pen pals, librarians, museum curators, younger children for whom he acts as teacher, customers for his small home business, music or art or dance instructors, a mentor with whom he could be an apprentice, anyone with whom your child shares learning or from whom your child learns. All activities that involve such other people focus both on educational goals and objectives and on socialization.

Any potential challenge to your right to home school that may be based upon the socialization issue might be satisfactorily counteracted with the development of lessons involving such a learning community. In addition, consider including interesting biographies in your lessons — during literature time, but also with other subject areas, such as social studies, science, and math. Those biographies about people who have contributed significantly to or exhibited sensitivity to the welfare of the community, of human society globally, and of the environment would be considered most applicable to the development of socialization skills. You might also make special effort to design lessons which involve your child in citizenship activities and cooperative game-playing.

Be sure to document those activities which involve socialization — a lesson plan book in which you have recorded the planned activities, or a home-teacher's daily log, and a curriculum which includes some socialization-related goals and objectives. If socialization is an issue of great concern in your local school district or state, you may wish to maintain a separate "socialization log" in which you date, describe, and potentially even evaluate your socialization-related learning activities.

The fourth issue raised at the beginning of this chapter involved what might be perceived of as a conflict: How can you teach (if you wish) in an unstructured fashion or let your lessons be child-directed if your written curriculum is structured?

In an attempt to answer this often-asked question, perhaps we could think of your curriculum as analogous to a multi-storied building with as many floors as you have subjects to teach. The building itself is a sound structure, elevators transport you between floors and hallways lead you from door to door. The doors are numbered in consecutive or sequential fashion, and the rooms throughout the building are unique in their accouterments but similar in overall arrangement. In other words, there is structure, there is order, their is a planned arrangement. However, the people who enter and move about in the building are free to go wherever they want or need to go in the building. They move from floor to floor, sometimes ride back and forth between floors, enter only those floors and doors they want to enter or are ready to enter, interact with other people in the building as desired or as beneficial, and so on. The people and their movement are not structured, unless structure is self-imposed; they do things in an orderly fashion only to the extent they wish; they may follow the arrangement precisely or roam about more freely.

The important factor with respect to the building itself is that it is indeed orderly, structured. Its arrangement assists people. It helps them find their way.

Thus it is with a curriculum. It is an orderly guide. As you and your child translate your curriculum into lessons, you, like the people in the building, are free to follow the structure as precisely or as loosely as you see fit while the contents and arrangement of your curriculum assist you in finding your way day-by-day, week-by-week, and eventually year-by-year. You may roam freely from floor to floor; you may remain in any one room on any one floor longer than in other rooms and on other floors. The option is yours. If your child's interest, for instance, is greatest in art, you may let art dominate your lessons. If you feel music instruction is not as relevant as other subject areas, you may elect to teach music for just a few weeks each semester or during just one or two days' lessons each week. If you are more able to teach literature than any other subject, you may allow literature to enter every "floor," every subject area by designing lessons that include much literature. If outdoor education attracts you and your child, open the windows, open the doors, let the building wait for your return while you hold lessons "in the field." However, you will want to temper your yen to roam to some extent, that extent necessary for you to in time return to your overall plans for the day, week, month, or year.

Nevertheless, your lessons may take you and your child where you wish, in whatever fashion you wish, and accompanied by whatever materials you wish, while your home-written curriculum cues you to directions and focuses and emphases...thanks to its structure.

Postscript

USING THIS YEAR'S CURRICULUM TO WRITE NEXT YEAR'S CURRICULUM
An Easy Shift into Second Gear

If you intend to home school your child beyond one year, each new home-school year you will need to write a more advanced curriculum. The thought of repeating the curriculum-writing experience year-after-year may make you hesitate. But take heart! Each successive curriculum, at least through grade eight, will be easier to write than the first because you can use each curriculum you write as a foundation for the next. The same is true of the documents you develop to verify your use of your child's curriculum. Once you have designed each document, the design task is complete and won't need to be repeated. Thereafter, you will simply need to continue maintaining each document from year to year.

While this year you should read carefully and work through every chapter in this book, next year you can begin by reading pages 91-92, which explain how one year's curriculum may borrow goals and objectives from the previous year's curriculum...without repeating lessons. Then go to your file box to review and adjust File Copy A, File Copy B, and Worksheet 3. After that, reread and work through Chapter 4 with your previous year's curriculum in hand. Use the working copy of your old curriculum as a rough draft of the new — cross out fully achieved goals and objectives, leave those that need either expansion or further practice, and add more advanced goals and objectives. You may also have decided with a review of Worksheet 3 to delete and/or add a subject area or two. Use Chapter 4 to develop additions and to integrate them into your new curriculum. Incidentally, you may follow this procedure even if your previous year's curriculum was a purchased one. In other words, you could use one year's commercial curriculum as the springboard or rough copy from which you design your own curriculum for the new year.

Next, refer to Chapter 5 to revise and refine your rough curriculum until you arrive at a final copy of the new year's curriculum. Revisit Chapter 6 to locate textbooks and materials for your new "Textbooks and Materials" list. You'll be all set then for your child's new home-school year and the cost of your curriculum will be just as low-cost/no-cost as the previous year's curriculum.

Look over the records you kept the previous year to document your use of your child's curriculum. Any changes needed? Any records you want to add to those you already keep? If so, create them. If not, simply continue to date your records as you go and maintain them as you did the year before.

Each home-school year from now on will find you able to easily revamp your old year's curriculum in order to write the current year's curriculum — and each time for free. When your children reach high school age, courses may become more precisely defined and divergent from one another. At that point you will very likely need to make major adjustments in your old curriculum. The areas that are likeliest to continue in reasonable sequence are music, art, English/language arts, and physical education. Those which will become defined in isolation are the science, social studies, math, and vocational courses, and perhaps by the eleventh grade the English/language arts courses. At that point, continue to follow the procedures presented in this book, but seek additional help, as needed, course by course. Look to those sources of help noted on pp. 47-48. Again, solicit the help of your student too!

By the time your child reaches home-school high school, you'll be feeling like an expert at curriculum development. You and your child will have enjoyed several home-school years working on curricula and daily lessons that truly have meaning for you, that stem from your own philosophies and lifelong aims, that suit your child's learning needs, abilities, interests, and style better than any other curriculum could. You will both have a right to feel proud, as student and teacher, that you put forth the effort to write a low-cost/no-cost curriculum in the first place. You're also likely to feel exceedingly enriched by the year-by-year results of your home-written home curriculum.

Appendix A

K-6 Subject Area Breakdown

The following breakdown of the most common grades K-6 subject areas is not a curriculum. Instead, the breakdown provides a list of typical categories from which a home educator may develop goals and objectives — carefully selected according to their appropriateness for her particular home-school child. Those goals and objectives will then constitute the child's curriculum.

The breakdown does not intentionally reflect anyone's educational philosophies and aims, nor any student's abilities, needs, interests, and learning styles. These elements will need to be carefully considered by you as you develop your child's curriculum.

The terms used to identify main subject area headings in the breakdown are variable. For example, what is called "earth and space" in one list, may be noted as "solar system," "earth science," "physical geography," "astronomy," etc., in others. Or all of these terms may be lumped together under the one heading "science." Therefore, vary the subject area headings as you see fit when writing your own curriculum. You may, for example, elect to check your local school curriculum and duplicate its headings as appropriate — without sacrificing your freedom to design your curriculum as you wish.

Remember, too, that a curriculum must be sequential; i.e., arranged from the basic to the advanced. The breakdown below, however, is not entirely sequential. Instead, you'll find several sequential clusters within each section. For example, in the oral communication section you'll find a story comprehension cluster composed of 1) oral comprehension, 2) retelling read-aloud stories, 3) telling anecdotes, and 4) telling the "story" behind artwork. Likewise you'll find an oral vocabulary cluster of three items, a larger speech cluster, and others. If you select those items noted for your child's grade level, you will have a sequential list with which to work.

Realize, too, that continued practice in skills and knowledge learned during earlier years is frequently beneficial to a student, sometimes essential to his owning those skills and that knowledge for a lifetime. In addition, some activities indeed have unending value in the child's learning. Therefore, you'll discover below that many goal categories are carried from year to year. This does not mean that you would want to bore a first grader with learning activities he first completed in kindergarten. It just means you'll want to design new, more sophisticated learning activities which allow you to provide your child with continued, expanded practice and experience with some skills and knowledge. For example, the "telling anecdotes" category of the oral communications segment of reading is a category that should be continued throughout your youngster's schooling years. By telling anecdotes your child is practicing many skills useful to him as he develops academically. At all levels anecdotes help him to sharpen his use of English sentence structure, new vocabulary, vivid diction, vocal expressiveness, accuracy in conveying messages, and awareness of his audience. He will further be learning the structure of an anecdote, which transfers eventually to the structure of a children's story — an oral communications/written communications link. Telling anecdotes is an important activity for a child's academic development in oral communications, grammar, reading, and writing...important at all levels.

We also know that children usually learn *bits* about a subject area one year and add more *bits* the next. The subject and goals may, therefore, remain the same while the information itself changes. In the study of history, for instance, a kindergarten child may simply learn to note that there is an historical American holiday called "Thanksgiving" to which he attaches in his mind the figures of pilgrims, Indians, and turkeys. In first grade, this holiday is still a part of his history curriculum, but now he learns about the Mayflower, the idea of giving thanks, the feast as an event, and the concepts of discovery and religious freedom. Then in second grade, he may analyze the contents of the Mayflower's hold and learn about the trials and travails of ship travel for the pilgrims. In third grade perhaps the pilgrims' settlement and the important role the Indians played in their survival will dominate his history lessons about Thanksgiving. In the fourth grade, he may extend the meaning of this historical event to the harvest season everywhere and to the present time. And on he goes, learning about the same historical holiday for several years, but gaining more knowledge each year. Repetition is not the focus. Expansion of knowledge is.

So now as you look at the K-6 Subject Area Breakdown below, you'll note developmental areas and goal categories that may be taught at several grade levels. You'll know that it's okay to include those areas and categories even if they've been taught before to your child, but that expanded practice and/or new material will be covered at the new grade level.

You will, however, want to think carefully about your individual child and about which goal categories you should keep from his earlier learning. For example, if as a new first grader his auditory discrimination is excellent, perhaps you'll drop that category from your child's reading curriculum. However, if rhyme recognition was only lightly practiced by your former kindergartner, you may want to reuse that category in his first grade curriculum. What appears below in the breakdown is a roster of those goal categories which *typically* remain important at each level, as well as new goal categories for each level. You have the wonderful flexibility at home of sifting through what is typical to find just what is desirable for your unique child!

READING

The reading segment below consists of five developmental areas: oral communication, phonics/decoding, comprehension, fluency, and literature. While reading is one of the language arts, it is most often listed separately in home-school course requirements, and is, therefore, treated separately here. Note, too, that in some state requirements, *reading* refers only to phonics/decoding, comprehension, and fluency. Your child will, however, be provided a fuller reading curriculum if you include the oral communication and literature components. Research demonstrates that in our natural sequence of learning to read, oral communication experiences pave the way to reading skills, and literature experiences provide varied reading and enrichment. Remember, too, that the selection of literature is up to you when the time comes for daily lessons. You'll be fully free to include readings that reflect your philosophies and lifelong aims for your child.

Oral Communication

Leisure listening - song lyrics, storytelling, story and poetry readings, etc.	K 1 2 3 4 5 6
Listening for increased lengths of time with focused attention	K 1 2 3 4 5 6
Auditory discrimination (words that rhyme, alike and different sounds)	K 1
Giving and responding to 3-step directions	K 1
Oral comprehension (e.g., story sequences, remembering details, predicting outcomes, using appropriate verbal expression as one reads aloud)	K 1 2 3
Retelling stories that have been read aloud by the teacher	K 1 2 3
Telling anecdotes	K 1 2 3 4 5 6
Explaining the "story" behind one's own artwork, others' artwork, and photographs	K 1 2 3 4 5 6
Asking and responding to who, what, where, when, why and how questions	1 2 3 4 5 6
Using complete sentences while speaking	1 2 3
Using sentence variety	1 2 3 4 5 6

	K	1	2	3	4	5	6
Using past, present, and future verb tenses		1	2	3			
Using verb tenses appropriately in declarative, exclamatory, and interrogatory statements			2	3	4	5	6
Using the conditional forms of verbs (could, would, should)			2	3	4	5	6
Using possessive pronouns (e.g., my, mine, yours, his)			2	3	4	5	6
Using contractions, including future tense contractions			2	3	4	5	6
Using prepositions (e.g., in, on, at, over, until, of, between, beneath)			2	3	4	5	6
Recognizing the value of communication	K	1	2	3	4	5	6
Recognizing the diversity of communication	K	1	2	3	4	5	6
Using vocabulary related to common societal elements (e.g., modes of transportation, household items, kinds of buildings, descriptors of weather, clothing items, elements of nature, time words)	K	1	2	3			
Exploration of uses of words with several meanings		1	2	3	4	5	6
Appropriate use of common American idioms, cliches, metaphors					4	5	6
Listening for main ideas, details, sequence of events or steps in a process		1	2	3	4	5	6
Listening to answer questions or to formulate questions and reach conclusions		1	2	3	4	5	6
Critical listening					4	5	6
Interviewing					4	5	6
Interactive communication (unstructured, informal discussion with varying numbers of others)	K	1	2	3			
Oral problem solving (using discussion to solve a common problem)	K	1	2	3	4	5	6
Listening carefully to others opinions; expressing differences of opinion in a confident, yet sensitive, manner			2	3	4	5	6
Interactive communication including at times leadership of discussions, both listening skills and speaking skills, and conversational courtesy; sometimes in structured, formal situations					4	5	6

READING

Summarizing and clarifying group discussions		4	5	6
Effective expression and clarity of content in various speaking situations		4	5	6
Using gestures as a means of communication and interpreting those of others		4	5	6
Articulation and intonation in varied speaking situations			5	6
Using eye contact effectively in varied speaking/listening situations			5	6
Presenting brief "speeches" (e.g. show and tell)	K 1 2			
Presenting brief oral reports	2 3 4			
Giving introductions and announcements, telling stories, role-playing, and doing impersonations		3 4	5	6
Exploring the use of dramatic techniques — body, face, eyes, voice			5	6
Selecting appropriate topics for a particular speaking situation, gearing speech to the intended audience and for the intended purpose, using effective evidence and supporting information appropriate to the topic				6
Using visual aids as appropriate during speaking situations				6
Choral speaking or reading	2 3 4			
Presenting skits	2 3 4 5 6			
Creative dramatics	3 4 5 6			
Reading aloud and reciting poems			5	6
Identifying famous speakers and speeches and enjoying taped or live speeches of various types			5	6

Phonics/Decoding

Recognizing student's own written name	K
Recognizing upper/lower case letters in order and at random	K 1
Recognizing the connection between written symbols (letters and words on page) and the oral reading of those symbols	K 1

	K	1	2	3	4	5	6
Making letter-sound associations: single consonants and vowels, vowel combinations, consonant combinations		1	2				
Using letter-sound associations to decode one-syllable and two-syllable words		1	2				
Using prefixes and suffixes to decode words		1	2				
Recognizing root words as an aid to decoding		1	2				
Recognizing compound words as an aid to decoding		1	2				
Expanding sight word recognition		1	2	3			
Using context clues to decode unfamiliar words		1	2	3			
Independently using word recognition skills — phonics, word parts, sight words, context clues					4	5	6

Comprehension

	K	1	2	3	4	5	6
Reading stories to remember and understand		1	2	3	4	5	6
Functional reading — simple informative passages, directions, notes, recipes, etc.		1	2	3	4	5	6
Reading to remember and understand poetry, nonfiction, short plays			2	3	4	5	6
Identifying the sequence of events in a story	K	1	2	3	4	5	6
Remembering details in a story	K	1	2	3	4	5	6
Using expression during oral reading that reflects an understanding of the lines being read		1	2	3			
Making predictions (What might happen next?)		1	2	3			
Relating events in a story to real life events			2	3	4	5	6
Discussing cause and effect in a story			2	3	4	5	6
Applying problem-solving strategies to predicaments that occur in stories			2	3	4	5	6
Comparing and contrasting events in one story with events in another story				3	4	5	6
Recognizing figures of speech					4	5	6
Interpreting meaning when it is not directly stated						5	6
Identifying attributes or traits, motives, and feelings of characters in stories						5	6

READING

Composing orally or in writing a character sketch by synthesizing the noted traits of the character					5	6
Drawing common elements from two or more stories together; synthesizing them in a discussion or writing about the commonalities					5	6
Discussing sequence of events and characterization in short plays		2	3	4	5	6
Identifying subject and mood in poetry		2	3	4	5	6
Reading to expand one's own knowledge	1	2	3	4	5	6
Sharing information found in nonfiction readings	1	2	3	4	5	6
Recognizing and remembering topic and main idea of nonfiction readings	1	2	3	4	5	6
Answering who, what, where, when, why, and how questions regarding the details of nonfiction readings	1	2	3	4	5	6
Discussing nonfiction authors' purposes and views		2	3	4	5	6
Drawing conclusions and making inferences based upon nonfiction readings		2	3	4	5	6
Identifying poem, play, fiction, nonfiction, short story, novel, reference book				4	5	6
Adjusting reading methods to different reading materials and one's purposes for reading them					5	6

Fluency

Reading with a flowing left-to-right eye movement	1	2	3	4	5	6
Silent reading for understanding	1	2	3	4	5	6
Silent reading for comfortable but increasing speed, without sacrificing comprehension	1	2	3	4	5	6
Reading aloud at a smooth pace	1	2	3	4	5	6
Reading aloud with appropriate vocal expression	1	2	3	4	5	6

Literature

	K	1	2	3	4	5	6
Listening with interest to stories for pleasure	K	1	2	3	4	5	6
Spending alone, quiet time "reading" picture books	K	1	2				
Developing the habit of reading as a lifelong skill and pleasure	K	1	2	3	4	5	6
Selecting children's literature to take home from the library	K	1	2	3	4	5	6
Enjoying children's literature depicted in movies, television shows, puppet shows, stage plays	K	1	2	3	4	5	6
Distinguishing reality from fantasy	K	1	2	3			
Responding to stories in various ways: music, puppetry, skits, reenactments, readings, discussion, etc.	K	1	2	3	4	5	6
Creating artwork depicting characters and events in stories that have been read		1	2	3			
Using children's books as models for creating storybooks of one's own		1	2	3			
Exploring the feelings and emotions of story characters	K	1	2	3	4	5	6
Empathizing with characters in predicaments	K	1	2	3	4	5	6
Identifying story situations in which words are used to influence and/or manipulate characters				3	4	5	6
Understanding the terms "story," "character," "author," and "illustrator"	K	1	2				
Understanding the terms "event" and "ending" while discussing stories			2	3	4		
Understanding the terms "plot," "conflict," "suspense," and "metaphor"						5	6
Understanding the terms "mood" and "atmosphere" while discussing stories						5	6
Reading silently and aloud some of the "Easy to Read" children's books		1	2				
Comprehension activities with children's literature (as noted above)	K	1	2	3	4	5	6
Familiar story characters, authors, illustrators; establishing favorites	K	1	2	3	4	5	6
Expanding knowledge of familiar and favorite authors and their works			2	3	4	5	6

LANGUAGE ARTS

The language arts segment below includes seven areas: handwriting, mechanics of English usage, spelling, vocabulary, creative writing, language history. and library skills. Library skills may be woven into the above literature area; vocabulary may be taught in isolation or (and probably more wisely) integrated into lessons involving children's literature and other readings; and creative writing may become an extension of a child's experiences with literature. Even spelling and English usage may be linked to words and sentence structures found in a child's reading selections. However, for the sake of writing a curriculum in an expected, organized fashion, we place these areas here under the heading "language arts" simply because they are typically place here.

Handwriting

Holding crayons and pencils appropriately	K	1				
Tracing simple shapes	K	1				
Printing student's own name	K					
Printing upper and lower case letters	K	1				
Forming alphabet letters well while printing		1	2			
Writing numbers 1-100		1				
Frequently printing simple words and sentences (especially those the child is learning to read)		1	2	3		
Printing posters, captions on child's own artwork, signs, etc.		1	2	3		
Writing brief, functional notes to others			2	3		
Introduction to cursive writing			2	3		
Expanded practice at writing in cursive the words, phrases, and sentences the child has been learning to read					4 5 6	
Writing any/all numbers the child mentally recognizes			2	3	4 5 6	

Mechanics of English Usage

Orally practicing correct simple sentence structure (parent should be the model)	K	1	2	3			
Orally practicing correct English usage/ grammar (parent should be the model)	K	1	2	3	4	5	6
Exploring and practicing written sentence structure and usage/grammar		1	2	3	4	5	6
Understanding and orally using contractions, prepositions, personal and possessive pronouns		1	2	3	4	5	6
Using and responding to questions (who, what, where, when, why, how)		1	2	3			
Awareness of spoken English variances, (e.g. northern vs southern, formal vs. informal, occupational jargon, slang)			2	3	4		
Discussing and providing examples of spoken English variances					4	5	6
Reading with appropriate expression sentences that end with the period, exclamation point, and question mark.		1	2	3			
Reading with appropriate pauses the commas within sentences		1	2	3			
Using correctly in writing: period, exclamation point and question mark		1	2	3			
Use of the apostrophe in contractions found in the child's reading		1	2	3			
Capitalization of proper names, titles, and sentence beginnings		1	2	3			
Using commas correctly: in dates, in a series (e.g. red, blue, green, and yellow balloons), and commas of address (e.g. Mary, please come home.)			2	3	4		
Using quotation marks and underlining with titles			2	3	4		
In writing, correctly using contractions, prepositions, personal and possessive pronouns				3	4	5	6
Identifying and skillfully using nouns and verbs in varied forms				3	4	5	6
Identifying and skillfully using pronouns				3	4	5	6
Identifying and skillfully using adjectives and adverbs				3	4	5	6

LANGUAGE ARTS

Completing activities, as needed, in English grammar/usage textbooks to learn and practice usage skills not yet mastered	4 5 6
Referring to a usage/grammar handbook as needed when writing	4 5 6
Independently using correct punctuation and capitalization in varied written sentence forms	4 5 6
Independently using sentence structure and English usage/grammar appropriate to any given situation, informal to formal, oral and written	4 5 6

Spelling

Child's own name	K
Familiar names	K 1
Basic survival words and information (e.g., "help," child's address, phone number)	K 1 2
Color words and number words	1 2
One's own continually expanding reading vocabulary	1 2 3 4 5 6
One-syllable words, with single vowel, two medial vowels, and with medial vowel plus final *e*	1 2
One-syllable words that end in *-s* or *-ed*	1 2 3
Two-syllable words in the child's own reading vocabulary	2 3
Two-syllable words, with *-ing, -y, -er, -es, -ness, -less, -ful* endings and a continually expanding number of others	2 3 4 5 6
Any words which the child shows an interest in learning to spell	K 1 2 3 4 5 6
Contractions	2 3 4
Root words with their derivative spellings (e.g., play, playing, played, plays)	2 3 4 5 6
Compound words, especially those in one's own reading vocabulary	2 3 4 5 6
The rules for adding suffixes and prefixes to root words	4 5 6
Three- and four-syllable words and more difficult compound words	4 5 6

	K	1	2	3	4	5	6
Irregular spellings					4	5	6
Sound-alikes (both letters and words)					4	5	6
Ei/ie spellings and problematic endings					4	5	6
Words notoriously problematic for spellers					4	5	6

Vocabulary

	K	1	2	3	4	5	6
Much verbal interaction with others throughout daily life	K	1	2	3	4	5	6
Exposure to and use of an expanding oral vocabulary	K	1	2	3	4	5	6
Exploring the meanings of key words in storybooks	K	1	2				
Discussion of and defining together key words in children's stories prior to and after the reading		1	2	3	4	5	6
Follow-up oral, real-life exposure to key words in children's stories		1	2	3	4	5	6
Using context clues in reading selections or speech segments in order to infer unfamiliar word meanings		1	2	3	4	5	6
Basic reading vocabulary – words the young reader is learning to read and, therefore, which s/he needs to understand		1	2				
Basic writing vocabulary, stemming from reading vocabulary and life experiences		1	2				
Expanding reading vocabulary			2	3	4	5	6
Expanding oral vocabulary in conjunction with subject area studies, such as social studies, science, and math			2	3	4	5	6
Expanding writing vocabulary, based upon reading vocabulary, child's interests and experiences, and subject area studies			2	3	4	5	6
Using vivid words to describe sensory input		1	2	3	4	5	6
Using a thesaurus as an aid to accurate, vivid word choices				3	4	5	6
Oral and written exposure to varied forms of a word (e.g., foot, footing, footstep, football, foot locker, footboard, foothill, foothold, footpad, footprint, footsie)		1	2	3	4	5	6
Exploration of words related in meaning (e.g. cold, chilly, frosty, icy)		1	2	3	4	5	6
Exploration of words opposite in meaning		1	2	3	4	5	6

LANGUAGE ARTS

Exploration of the uses of words with many meanings	3 4 5 6
Expanding abstract word vocabulary (e.g., love, justice, righteousness, democracy)	3 4 5 6
Exploration of the emotive variance in words used to describe similar objects, events, or actions (e.g., Fido is a ...ball of fluff, pup, dog, mutt, mongrel, cur -OR- The man...crawls, shuffles, trudges, lumbers, marches, strides, struts.)	4 5 6
Reading and responding appropriately to emotive words	4 5 6
Using words according to their emotive qualities during varied forms of speaking and writing	4 5 6
Using emotive words in persuasive contexts (e.g. ads, political speeches, editorials, letters to editors)	5 6
Exposure to speech and reading which contain challenging vocabulary	5 6
Awareness of the power and influence that may be wielded in words (e.g., the influences words have on story characters, word use in advertisements)	3 4 5 6
Evaluating/analyzing the power and influence that may be wielded in words	5 6

Creative Writing

Many oral communication activities (as noted above)	K 1 2 3 4 5 6
Many literature activities (as noted above)	K 1 2 3 4 5 6
Telling anecdotes that are then written and read back to the student by someone else	K 1
Recognizing that writing is done because the writer has something to say; (e.g., a message to convey or story to relate)	1 2 3 4 5 6
Writing child's own brief stories	1 2 3 4
Writing brief descriptions and explanations	1 2 3 4
Writing steps in a process	3 4 5 6
Sharing with others one's own writings: stories, descriptions, explanations, and steps in a process	1 2 3 4 5 6

	K	1	2	3	4	5	6
Constructing "books" with child's own writings, as a means of "publishing"		1	2	3	4	5	6
The paragraph, its forms and development					4	5	6
Composition format — margins, indentations, neatness, etc.					4	5	6
Outlining					4	5	6
Idea generation — brainstorming, mapping related ideas, clustering ideas, etc.				3	4	5	6
Information gathering, discussion, etc., in order to mentally explore and develop a topic before writing about it				3	4	5	6
Identifying topic, audience, purpose for one's writing				3	4	5	6
Identifying one's own slant or angle, and form (e.g., poem, paragraph, story, report, etc.) as one prepares to write				3	4	5	6
Rough copy writing, including free writing (nonstop writing in rough form with no initial regard for mechanics or style)				3	4	5	6
Rough copy revising; sometimes asking for feedback on specified elements				3	4	5	6
Rough copy editing (e.g., grammar, punctuation, capitalization) with the benefit of feedback from another person or two				3	4	5	6
Diary writing or journal writing for oneself		1	2	3	4	5	6
Functional writing		1	2	3	4	5	6
Writing friendly letters					4	5	6
Writing brief business letters						5	6
Writing simple biographical sketches							6
Persuasive writing							6
Writing from varying points of view					4	5	6
Writing in a variety of forms, on a variety of topics, for a variety of purposes, and to various audiences				3	4	5	6
Writing as a regular activity for uninterrupted periods of time		1	2	3	4	5	6
Writing as a leisure-time activity	K	1	2	3	4	5	6
Appreciation for and consciousness of the cadences, humor, images created by the words one uses					4	5	6
Writing plays					4	5	6
Writing poetry					4	5	6

LANGUAGE ARTS

Much observation and exploration of the sensory details of scenes and events which are then brought to the writing table	1 2 3 4 5 6
Discussion of moods in real life events and circumstances	3 4 5 6
Locating information, reading for information, and then writing briefly about the researched topic	3 4 5 6
Independently organizing ideas and information for writing	5 6
Independently writing rough compositions with emphasis on content (rather than form, style, and mechanics)	5 6
Diction — selecting words wisely, with consideration especially for their emotive variances (e.g., pet, puppy, dog, mutt, mongrel, cur)	5 6
Revising for clarity, coherence, and unity	5 6
Editing for spelling, punctuation, capitalization, usage/grammar, and overall format (e.g., indentions, margins)	5 6
Independently preparing polished, final drafts appropriate to the writer's audience and purpose	5 6
Awareness of writing as an occupational field	6

Language History

Awareness that the English language, like all languages, has a history	4 5
The totally oral nature of the earliest actual language; that is, means of mutual communication among people	4 5
Early written symbols — pictographs, abstract symbols, early alphabets	4 5 6
Early mediums for making those symbols — natural paints and chalks, sticks and stones, rock walls, animal skins, etc.	4 5 6
Papyrus as the first "paper"	5 6
The continually changing nature of language	5 6

Ways in which new words have entered and do enter the English language						6
The concept of the language as "living" in oral form vs. the static and therefore insufficient nature of written records of language use and standards						6
The need for standards of use for any language (e.g., standard spelling and grammar) regardless of the changing nature of language						6

Library Skills

Book care	K	1	2			
Locating fiction and nonfiction books in a library	K	1	2			
Understanding the functions of a librarian	K	1	2			
Book selection and checking out books	K	1	2			
Using a card catalog or computer catalog				3 4 5 6		
Identifying and using the parts of a book (e.g., index, table of contents, chapters, glossary, appendix, title page, copyright page)				3 4 5 6		
Using varied written materials to locate and gather information				3 4 5 6		
Basic reference books and correlated use-skills — dictionary, atlas, thesaurus, encyclopedia				3 4 5 6		
Library media (e.g., cassette tapes, filmstrips, films, slides, video tapes)				3 4 5 6		
Library research				4 5 6		
Reading reference books and using formatted cues (e.g., guide words atop dictionary pages; ABC order, abbreviations),					5 6	
Reading to gather and organize information (skimming-outlining, questioning, reading-notetaking, rereading)					5 6	
Awareness of community and key state newspapers					5 6	
Identification of state and special libraries					4 5	
Awareness of the Library of Congress						6
Introduction to the history of book making and of libraries						6

MATHEMATICS

Included in the math segment are seven areas: patterns, number system, geometry, measurement, computation and problem solving, and computers. *Much* exploration of patterns should be emphasized in the preschool stages and primary grades as a precursor to recognizing and understanding numerical patterns of all sorts. In fact, you'll note below that exploration and awareness are the foundation processes of math studies (as well as science and other studies). The youngest learners begin with these processes, graduate into higher level thinking and physical processes, such as hypothesis and problem solving. Why? — simply because the youngest learners are not naturally capable of higher level thinking and processing. A good curriculum allows for a child's natural abilities and stage of mental development.

While computer literacy is becoming more and more important in all aspects of American life, it is still not always included in public school curriculums. However, because computer education is becoming more and more common, computer literacy is included here.

All math categories can be integrated into lessons involving other subject areas. Measurement skills can be used in science, for example, and geometry skills in art. Patterns and the number system itself are integral to music, and computers skills are especially useful with creative writing. Computation and problem solving skills can be applied in many of these and other academic and practical situations.

Patterns

Frequently exploring, recognizing, and creating simple patterns, and then increasingly complex patterns in a variety of modes with a variety of objects	K	1	2	3
Recognition of same/different 1-10 numerals	K			
Recognition of same/different 1-100 numerals		1		
Recognition of same/different 1-1000 numerals			2	
Verbally describing visible patterns		1	2	3

Number System

Identifying 0-10 in order and at random	K		
Placing and reciting 0-10 in numerical order	K		
Counting objects 0-10	K		
Matching a set of objects with the appropriate number	K	1	2
Estimating and identifying two to three sets of objects as "greater than" and "less than"	K	1	
Identifying 0-20 numerals in order and at random		1	
Placing and reciting 0-20 in order		1	
Determining the order of any given set of numbers between 0 and 20		1	
Reciting numbers backwards 20 to 0		1	2
Counting objects 0-20		1	
Writing a number in varied forms (e.g., 6, 5 + 1, 3 + 3, 7 -1, 10 - 4, etc.)		1 2	3
Place value (ones, tens, hundreds)		1	2
Reciting 0-100 by tens		1	
Reading and writing number words to "twenty"		1	
Ordinals, "first" to "twentieth"		1	
Identifying what number "comes next"		1	
Identifying which of two to three sets of objects has "one more than" and "one less than"		1	2
Awareness of numbers in real-life settings		1	2
Counting objects 0-100		1	2
Determining the order of any given set of numbers between 0 and 100		1	2
Identifying numerals 0-1000 in order and at random		2	3
Placing 0-1000 in numerical order		2	3
Reciting 0-1000 by tens		2	3
Reading and writing number words to one-hundred		2	3
Ordinals, "first" to "hundredth"		2	3
Writing and Reading 1/2, 1/4, 1/8		2	3

MATHEMATICS

Expanding recognition, reading, and writing of numbers as far into the number range as the student can handle	3	4	5	6
Rounding numbers, regrouping numbers		4	5	6
Identifying prime and composite numbers		4	5	6
Listing the factors of a number		4	5	6
Identifying and expanding number patterns		4	5	6
Comparing and ordering fractions to 1/16th		4	5	6
Determining missing elements in pictographic and numerical patterns				6
Creating patterns, given a formal rule; and developing formal rules for patterns				6
Translating sets into numbers and numbers into sets				6
Roman numerals				6
The metric system				6

Geometry

Exploring shapes and shape patterns	K	1		
Identifying the four basic shapes: circle, triangle, rectangle, square	K	1		
Classifying, grouping the four basic shapes	K	1	2	
Locating examples of the four basic shapes in the real world	K	1	2	
Verbally describing the four basic shapes and their properties		2	3	4
Identifying, classifying, and grouping additional shapes: cube, sphere, cone, pyramid, cylinder, and rectangular solids		1	2	3
Recognizing shapes and figures as "same" or "different"		1	2	
Sorting varied geometric shapes and other objects		1	2	3
Creating increasingly complex patterns with simple shapes		1	2	3
Comparing and contrasting a wide variety of simple and complex shapes and figures		2	3	4
Position terms, such as: inside, outside, beneath, above, alongside		1	2	3
Symmetry and asymmetry		1	2	3

Geometric terms: point, line, line segment, ray, parallel lines, perpendicular lines	4	5	6
Classifying angles and triangles, quadrilaterals, and other polygons	4	5	6
Term: coordinate plane	4	5	6
Making constructions in a plane using compass and straightedge	4	5	6
Sketching and constructing geometric shapes and relationships	4	5	6
Measuring shapes	4	5	6
Solving problems involving geometric shapes and their properties and relationships to each other		5	6

Measurement

Exploring length and weight	K	1	2	
Understanding and using these terms: longer, shorter, heavier, lighter	K	1	2	
Estimating longer, shorter, heavier, lighter between two objects	K	1	2	3
Using nonstandard means of measuring comparable lengths and weights (e.g., using toothpicks to measure pencil lengths)	K	1	2	
Beginning to understand: day, week, month, year	K			
Recognizing the clock as a tool that measures time	K			
Recognizing a penny, nickel, and dime and understand the term "money"	K			
Using a calendar to recognize days, weeks, months, year		1	2	3
Using a clock to tell time to the nearest minute		1	2	3
Estimating and measuring the passage of time			2	3
Understanding and using the terms "inch" and "foot"		1	2	
Using a 12-inch ruler to measure lengths		1	2	
Understanding and using the term "degrees" of temperature		1	2	
Using a thermometer to compare temperatures of liquids		1	2	3

MATHEMATICS

Using a thermometer to log daily outdoor air temperatures	1 2 3
Using various lenses to observe objects	1 2 3
Using measuring spoons and cups in simple cookery	1 2 3
Recognizing quarters, half-dollars, and one-dollar bills	1 2
Using pennies, nickels, dimes to make purchases (for play or for real)	1 2
Understanding and using the term "yard"	2 3
Using a 36-inch ruler to measure lengths	2 3
Using non-standard measures of lengths greater than 36 inches	3 4
Estimating, determining, and comparing the costs of more than one item for sale	2 3 4
Using pennies, nickels and dimes to make purchases and estimate change	2 3 4
Estimating which of two irregular shapes has the greater area	2 3 4
Frequently estimating measurements of various sorts and then verifying accuracy by using standard means of measuring	4 5 6
Frequently comparing and contrasting measurements	5 6
Use of square units, cubic units, varied rulers, protractors, and varied scales to measure area, perimeter, volume, and angles	5 6
Circumference and surface area measurements	5 6
Liquid capacity	5 6
Reading and constructing tables and graphs, first simple and gradually more sophisticated	5 6
Using tables and graphs for making comparisons	5 6
Using calculators and computers to generate tables and graphs	5 6
Using tables, graphs and direct means of measurement in practical/functional life situations to make decisions	5 6

	1	2	3	4	5	6
Arranging statistical information in ascending and descending order						6
Determining mean, median, and range, given statistical information						6
Using statistical information to recognize trends and predict future results						6

Computation and Problem Solving

	1	2	3	4	5	6
Basic addition facts to 10	1					
Basic subtraction facts to 10	1					
The symbols: +, –, =	1					
Use of "counting on," "counting up to," and "counting down from"	1					
Both horizontal and vertical addition and subtraction	1					
Addition of three one-digit numbers	1					
Identifying 1/2 and 1/4 of a divisible object	1	2				
Writing 1/2 and 1/4 as recognized sections of a divisible object	1	2				
Math in everyday problem-solving situations	1	2	3	4	5	6
Verbally explaining processes used to solve problems			3	4	5	6
Reading and interpreting simple bar, circle, line, or picture graphs	1	2	3			
Creating simple bar graphs which compare two, then three, then four groups	1	2	3	4		
Addition and subtraction facts to 100		2				
Adding two, three, or more numbers		2	3	4	5	6
Use of the calculator		2	3			
Basic multiplication facts		2	3			
The symbol: x		2				
Frequently practicing estimation of sums and differences		2	3			
Identifying 1/8 of a divisible object		2	3			
Writing 1/8 as a recognized section of a divisible object		2	3			
Addition and subtraction to 1000			3			
Rounding numbers			3	4		
Adding and subtracting fractions, including combinations with whole numbers				4	5	6

MATHEMATICS

Mental addition and subtraction of two-digit numbers and of fractions	4 5 6
Subtracting two- and three-digit numbers involving regrouping	4 5 6
Using estimation to determine the reasonableness of calculated answers	4 5 6
Frequently practicing estimation of products	4 5 6
Estimation of easily recognizable fractions and sizes of areas	4 5 6
Finding equivalent fractions	4 5 6
Solving problems with equivalent fractions	4 5 6
Developing problem-solving techniques for practical mathematical problems (e.g., consumer math)	4 5 6
Multiplication of one- and two-digit numbers and introduction to multiplying two-digit by three-digit numbers	5 6
Relating multiplication to division	4
Introductory division	4
Dividing multiples of 10, 100, and 1000	5 6
Dividing one- and two-digit divisors into one- to four-digit dividends	5 6
Determining when sums, differences, products, and quotients are even or odd	5 6
Introductory decimals	4
Frequently practicing estimation of sums, differences, products, and quotients — with whole numbers, fractions, decimals	5 6
Finding factors of numbers less than 20	5 6
Finding factors of numbers less than 200	5 6
Identifying prime numbers less than 100	5 6
Finding equivalent fractions and mixed number/fraction equivalents	5 6
Solving problems with equivalent fractions using addition, subtraction, multiplication, and division	5 6
Finding fractional parts of whole numbers mentally	5 6
Adding and subtracting like fractions mentally	5 6

Reading and writing decimals to thousandths				5	6	
Rounding decimals				5	6	
Identifying equivalent decimals				5	6	
Solving problems with equivalent decimals using addition, subtraction, multiplication, and division				5	6	
Comparing and ordering whole numbers, fractions, decimals				5	6	
Frequently estimating decimals				5	6	
Introductory ratios				5	6	
Determining ratios from models				5	6	
Solving problems involving ratios				5	6	
Introductory percents				5	6	
Translating percents into models					6	
Solving problems involving percents					6	
Expressing ratios as percents or as decimals					6	
Recognizing and using patterns of squares and cubes, and of exponents, powers, and roots					6	
Recognizing functions; and solving problems using functions					6	
Awareness of math-related occupational fields					6	

Computers

Basic computer terms: keyboard, monitor, screen, floppy disk, space bar, return key, boot	K	1					
Computer care; start up and shut down	K	1					
Simple keyboarding skills	K	1	2				
Computer use for fun	K	1	2	3	4	5	6
Number games	K	1	2				
Simple word processing (or child may observe)	K	1	2				
Awareness of computers in other people's lives and work	K	1	2	3			
Educational math programs			2	3	4	5	6
Problem-solving programs				3	4	5	6
Using a word processing program for entering, editing, and printing text				3	4	5	6

MATHEMATICS

Other educational software use	3 4 5 6
Observations of computers being used in occupational situations	4 5 6
Simple computer languages (e.g., Basic, Logo)	4 5 6
Basic computer programming	5 6
Understanding the diverse uses of computers — in individual lives, in business, in education, in science and technology, in industry, in the fine arts, etc.; also the limitations of computers and the role of programming in computer operation	6
Dealing with difficulties that arise during computer operation — typical techniques for solving or circumventing difficulties and using program manuals to deal with difficulties	6
Using a program manual tutorial to learn a new computer program	6
Using basic, essential system commands	5 6
Recognizing, using, and caring for peripheral devices	5 6
Data storage, search, retrieval, analysis, revision, and printout	6
Exploring basic computer graphics	6

SCIENCE

Included in the science segment below are nine areas, whose names, incidentally, may vary from curriculum to curriculum: scientific data gathering and scientific processes, meteorology, biology, earth and space, physics, chemistry, geology, environmental science, and oceanography. The *scientific data gathering and scientific processes* heading may not occur in many curriculums because *process* may be inherent in other segments or in some cases largely neglected. Inclusion of process goals here will help you consider them for inclusion in your curriculum. Likewise, the environmental science heading is becoming increasingly common, and for that reason is included below.

In elementary curriculums, all of the above headings may be lumped under the one heading: *science*. Most curriculums will include some general breakdown, such as the one used here. On the other hand, in some curriculums, the headings may be more specific. *Biology* may be stated separately as *zoology* and *botany*, for example. *Astronomy* may be the term used for space studies. *Ecology* may be listed in place of or adjacent to *environmental science* or *earth science*. Likewise, the headings may be less objective and instead reflect the framer's philosophies: Creation science, for instance, or conservation science. However, because the terms do vary from curriculum to curriculum, your selected headings are not likely to be challenged. If you want to make sure of this, you might find out what science course headings are used in your local school for children your child's age/grade and begin with those headings.

Remember again, as with all subjects, that your philosophies and aims for your child may be freely brought into your selection of science texts and materials and into your daily lesson activities, even if those philosophies and aims were not overtly apparent in your written curriculum. Creation science, for example, may not merely be mentioned in your headings, goals, or objectives, but may become in daily lessons the foundation of your entire science curriculum.

Scientific Data Gathering and Scientific Processes

Expressing and following one's innate curiosity about the world of nature and one's pleasure in and appreciation for nature	K	1	2	3	4	5	6
The five physical senses: touch, taste, smell, hearing, and sight	K	1					

	K	1	2	3	4	5	6
Concept that we learn about the world through our five physical senses	K	1					
Using the five senses to gather and collect data from the world of nature	K	1	2	3	4	5	6
Comparing objects according to their physical properties	K						
Comparing and contrasting the physical properties of objects and sets of objects		1	2				
Sorting and grouping objects according to their physical properties		1	2				
Arranging objects according to their properties, as from hottest to coldest, largest to smallest, roughest to smoothest, heaviest to lightest, etc.			2	3	4	5	6
Describing and citing examples of the tremendous diversity among living and among nonliving things	K	1	2				
Citing examples and describing the tremendous diversity of living and of nonliving things and also of the regularity, patterns, and order in nature				3	4	5	6
Observation as a scientific method	K	1	2	3			
Concept of exploration and investigation as scientific methods		1	2				
Viewing, examining and creating models of living and nonliving things		1	2	3			
The role of experimentation in science				3	4	5	6
Using basic science tools: magnifying glass, magnet, simple scale — for scientific exploration and experimentation		1	2	3			
The role science plays in meeting human needs				3	4	5	6
Prediction — using gathered data and/or known information to predict natural progressions, changes, or outcomes				3	4	5	6
Inference — inferring possible theories or explanations for natural circumstances, events, and changes				3	4	5	6
Verification of predictions and inferences				3	4	5	6
The roles of imagination and hypothesis in science				3	4	5	6
Describing sounds as to loudness, pitch, duration	K	1	2				

SCIENCE

	K	1	2	3	4	5	6
Identifying foods as sour, sweet, or salty	K	1	2				
Discriminating between matter that is liquid and solid	K	1	2				
Distinguishing between hotter and colder	K	1	2				
Identifying liquids, solids, and gases			2	3	4		
Exploring the effects of heat and cold on solids and liquids	K	1	2				
Describing and predicting the effects of heat and cold on solids and liquids				3	4	5	6
Using heat and cold to create desired change				3	4	5	6
Estimation of temperatures of varied matter, followed by verification			2	3	4		
Identifying changes in continually observed living and nonliving things			2	3	4		
Identifying causes and effects of observed changes					4	5	6
Comparing, contrasting, analyzing, determining cause and effect, inferring, predicting, and hypothesizing about a multitude of objects and sets of objects (living and nonliving) with regards to their physical properties and changes in their physical properties					4	5	6
Observing, identifying, measuring, and recording changes and the causes and effects of change using a variety of measurements and measuring tools						5	6
Scientific estimation of properties, measurements, outcomes and changes						5	6
Reception and response of living things to stimuli				3	4	5	6
Using science tools: microscope, stethoscope, telescope, for scientific exploration and experimentation				3	4	5	6
Importance of accuracy in scientific observation and means of recording observations					4	5	6
Awareness and observation of relationships among living things					4	5	6
Synthesizing gathered data or the results of varied experiments and drawing conclusions						5	6

The tentative nature of scientific knowledge and the need for repeated demonstration of scientific "fact"	3	4	5
How scientific concepts become accepted governing principles	3	4	5
Constructing diagrams and models to represent science concepts or events		4 5 6	
Identifying sources of scientific information		4 5 6	
Evaluating the reliability of sources of scientific information			5 6
Evaluating scientific information for its adequacy in relation to one's purpose			5 6
Distinguishing between valid and invalid and /or pertinent and nonpertinent data and information			5 6
Using known scientific data to develop a model of predictable outcomes or changes (e.g., using known applications of a natural insect repellent to predict results of a new application)		4 5 6	
Key people and science discoveries of the past that have affected scientific practice and thought today		4 5 6	
Tracing the development of a scientific discovery, process, thought, or technology		4 5 6	
The relationship and difference between science and technology (the one investigative, the other oriented towards the development of applications)		4 5 6	
Awareness of the interdependency of varied technologies		4 5 6	
Awareness of the tremendous utilitarian effects of technologies for humans		4 5 6	
Comparing and contrasting the lifestyles of people of the past and present to explain how science and resulting technologies have changed the way people live			5 6
Awareness of present technological limits			5 6
Awareness of technological effects on economic issues			5 6
Ongoing knowledge of current technological developments and events			5 6
Awareness of science-related occupational fields			6

Meteorology

	K	1	2	3	4	5	6
Awareness of elements, patterns, and changes in weather	K	1					
Identifying ways in which weather affects human activity and animal activity	K	1					
Awareness of ways people in the child's home area adapt to weather	K	1					
Exploring effects of weather on plants	K	1					
Describing ways weather alters the earth's appearance	K	1					
Using an outdoor thermometer	K	1					
Logging daily outdoor temperatures and weather conditions in child's home area		1					
Observing differences in temperature in relationship to elevation		1					
Weather-related human safety measures		1					
Awareness of typical weather patterns in other parts of the world and the fact that weather in varied parts of the world differs at any one time		1					
Ways people in various other parts of the world adapt to the weather		1					
Awareness of dramatic, potentially damaging weather systems			2	3	4		
Unusual, longer term weather conditions (e.g., monsoon, drought)					4	5	6
Ongoing consciousness of major, current weather systems around the globe					4	5	6
The evaporation cycle; clouds and precipitation					4	5	6
Weather forecasting			2	3	4		
Weather satellites and other weather instruments			2	3	4		
The seasons	K	1	2				
Characteristics of each season in child's home region	K	1	2				
The year by year predictability and variability of the seasons	K	1	2	3			
Seasonal animal activity	K	1	2	3			
The seasons and the life cycle of a plant		1	2	3	4		

How seasons vary in degree in various parts of the world				3	4	5	
Causes and effects of the seasons				3	4	5	6

Biology

Identification of plant life vs. non-plant life and nonliving things	K	1	2				
Identification of basic plant types: tree, bush, grass, etc.	K	1	2				
Recognition of similarities and differences in plants	K	1	2				
Identifying by name a growing number of specific types of plants, beginning with those in the child's home area	K	1	2	3	4	5	6
Basic external plant anatomy	K	1	2				
Seeds, cuttings, and plant growth cycle	K	1	2				
Survival needs of plants	K	1	2				
Basic systems of plants and their systemic functions		1	2	3			
Edible plants		1	2				
Poisonous and other harmful plant safety measures		1	2				
The relationship of plants to all other living things			2	3			
Unusual plants (e.g., Venus-flytrap)				3	4	5	6
Photosynthesis				3	4		
Identification of animal life vs. non-animal life and nonliving things	K	1	2				
Identification of commonly known animals	K	1	2				
Recognition of likenesses and differences in animals	K	1	2				
Identifying by name an increasing number of animals, beginning with those in the child's home area	K	1	2	3	4	5	6
Unusual animals (e.g., narwhal)				3	4	5	6
Basic external animal anatomy	K	1	2				
Basic needs of all animals	K	1	2				
Food chains		1	2	3			
Common animal homes, habits, and foods		1	2	3			
Animal communities		1	2	3			
Basic animal body functions (e.g., digestion)		1	2	3			

SCIENCE

	K	1	2	3	4	5	6
Concept of animal birth and growth	K	1	2	3			
Tracing life cycles of varied animals			2	3	4	5	6
Heredity			2	3	4	5	6
Stimuli and response				3	4	5	6
Natural competition of plants and animals				3	4	5	6
Adaptation and extinction				3	4	5	6
Interdependency of humans and animals with their environments (including both living and nonliving elements)			2	3	4	5	6
Basic external human anatomy	K	1	2	3			
Basic organs and systems within the human body and their systemic functions					4	5	6
Physical human growth and development					4	5	6
Nutrition in relationship to human growth					4	5	6
Cells as the basic unit of life; one-celled creatures; parts of a cell					4	5	6
Classifications of groups of varied living things, from the simple to the complex					4	5	6
Biological tools and technologies					4	5	6

Earth and Space

	K	1	2	3	4	5	6
The earth as man's physical home, a daily rotating sphere	K	1					
Identifying the sun, moon, and stars	K	1					
The sun's light and warmth as necessary for survival on earth		1	2				
The moon's relationship to the sun and earth with respect to the moon's source of light, its rotation and orbit		1	2				
Observing the changing shape and size of the moon throughout a month		1	2				
Reasons for the monthly changes in the moon; logging the phases of the moon			2	3			
The moon's size; its role as a satellite of the earth, its physical characteristics			2	3	4		
Causes of our day and night			2	3			
Varying lengths of day and night				3	4	5	
Awareness of the effects of night and day on biological systems, including that of humans (e.g., circadian rhythm)						5	6

Topic	K	1	2	3	4	5	6
Tides and their relationship to the moon						5	6
Solar and lunar eclipses; their predictability, causes, effects						5	6
The sun as a star		1	2				
The burning, gaseous composition of the sun, its size in comparison to the earth, and its distance from the earth		1	2	3	4		
The sun as earth's major source of energy				3	4		
Other stars — comparable sizes, composition, brightness, and constellations				3	4	5	6
Awareness of the earth as a planet and the existence of other planets, all of which orbit the sun		1	2				
The earth as the third planet; its size and distance from the sun				3	4		
Earth's rotation, orbit, axis, and tilt					4	5	6
Awareness of the solar system			2	3			
The known objects of the solar system and their relationships to one another				3	4	5	6
The comparative sizes of the planets, their compositions, temperatures, cyclical movements (rotation, orbit, axis, tilt, gravity, speed), characteristics, companions (e.g., moons and rings), and effects on one another				3	4	5	6
The universe; the vastness of "the unknown" in outer space; scientific instruments and techniques used to study and explore the known and unknown; planetariums					4	5	6
Galaxies					4	5	6
Awareness of space explorations and manned space travel	K	1	2	3	4		
Awareness of distance and time in space		1	2	3	4		
Basic rocketry					4	5	6
The history of America's space program					4	5	6
Atmosphere, composition and properties			2	3	4		
Air movement in the atmosphere			2	3	4		
Air quality — measures of, causes and effects, the constancy of change						5	6
Climate, types, and their ever-changing nature			2	3	4		

SCIENCE

	K	1	2	3	4	5	6
Major climate regions of the earth, climactic change, diversity, predictability, causes and effects						5	6
Gathering and exploring objects and data which demonstrate that the earth is made up of land, water, and rock, and is surrounded by air	K	1	2				
The importance of land, water, rock, and air to humans and to all other living things		1	2	3			
Awareness of natural phenomena, such as landslides, tidal waves, volcanoes, earthquakes, powerful storms		1	2	3			
Causes and effects of natural phenomena			2	3	4		
The earth's surface as ever-changing			2	3	4		
The earth's crust and its layers			2	3	4		
The ozone layer — our natural sun shield; the positive effects of large forests on the ozone layer; the negative effects of air pollution on the ozone layer; the danger to humans and other living things of too much heat from the sun						5	6

Physics

	K	1	2	3	4	5	6
Exploration of energy, motion and force	K	1	2				
Force as a push or pull			2	3			
Magnitude and direction of force, work, power					4	5	6
Friction and gravity			2	3	4	5	
Simple machines and their uses					4	5	
How simple machines are used to create more complex machines					4	5	6
Exploration of sound and light	K	1	2				
Sound and light as forms of energy			2	3			
The nature, production, characteristics, and effects of sound			2	3	4	5	6
Exploration of magnetic force	K	1	2				
Study of magnetic force				3	4	5	6
The earth's magnetic poles; the compass; magnetic storms					4	5	6
Awareness of the nature, sources, characteristics, and effects of light					4	5	6

	K	1	2	3	4	5	6
Awareness of wave energy and its practical applications					4	5	6
Static electricity				3	4	5	
Awareness of conductivity					4	5	
Awareness of electrical circuits and electrical production, power, and use					4	5	6
Electrical storms						5	6
The practical applications of mechanical energy, electricity, and magnetism					4	5	6
Means of measuring energy				3	4	5	
Heat transfer				3	4	5	
Practical uses of heat energy				3	4	5	6
Practical uses of kinetic energy				3	4	5	6
Awareness of nuclear energy and radioactivity and their practical uses						5	6

Chemistry

	K	1	2	3	4	5	6
Exploration of the composition and properties of substances	K	1	2	3			
Measuring and classifying substances by their properties			2	3	4	5	6
Solids, liquids and gases, and their properties and ability to be changed			2	3	4	5	6
The interaction of energy with matter to create change				3	4	5	6
Solutions and materials that dissolve				3	4	5	6
Awareness of practical uses of chemical compounds and mixtures (e.g., medicines, cleansers)				3	4	5	6
Freezing, melting, condensation, boiling, evaporation					4	5	6
Basic atomic structure of matter					4	5	6
Awareness that all matter consists of elements which have specific properties; compounds; mixtures					4	5	6
Measuring, classifying, describing matter by mass, length, volume						5	6
Introductory crystals						5	6
Introduction to acids, bases, and salts						5	6

Geology

Exploration of rocks	K	1	2			
Informal sorting and grouping of rocks by varied physical properties (e.g., color, size, shape, degree of hardness, beauty)	K	1	2			
Awareness of practical uses of rocks			2	3	4	
Exposure to gem stones and their aesthetic and other properties					4 5 6
Minerals					4 5 6
Rock and mineral identification, properties and formation					4 5 6
Composition of earth as rocks and minerals				4	5 6
Soil formation, quality and properties					5 6
Erosion					5 6
Forces that cause continual changes in land and in bodies of water					5 6
Geologic pressure and the resulting land-forms and phenomena					5 6
Awareness of tectonic plates and the cause of earthquakes and volcanoes					5 6
Awareness of historical changes in the earth's crust					5 6
Awareness of fossils as a "recorder" of geologic and biologic history					5 6
Limits of earth's natural geologic resources					6

Oceanography

Awareness of the vastness of the oceans		1	2	3	4	
Identification and locations of oceans and ratio of continents to oceans on earth					4 5 6
Properties and composition of oceans					4 5 6
Awareness of tides, causes and effects, variability, predictability					4 5 6
Effects of oceans on climate					4 5 6
Awareness of tools and technologies used to study and explore the oceans					4 5 6
Ocean currents and their effects					5 6
Waves, causes, variability, and unusual phenomena, such as tidal waves					5 6

Storms at sea (e.g., hurricane)						5	6
Awareness of the diverse plant and animal life in oceans and tide pools						5	6

Environmental Science

Ways natural resources are used to meet peoples' needs	K	1	2				
Concept of multiple use of natural resources			2	3	4		
Concepts of overuse and of pollution	K	1	2				
Examples of overuse and of pollution in the child's home area		1	2	3	4		
Concept of human responsibility for environmental preservation/conservation	K	1	2	3	4	5	6
Identification of several man-made products or industrial byproducts that pollute; and those that avoid or reduce pollution		1	2	3			
Effects of polluted air and water on plants, animals, and humans		1	2	3			
Concept of environmental balance			2	3	4		
The interdependency of living things and their environment (consisting of living and nonliving elements)			2	3	4		
Concept of endangered plants and animals	K	1	2				
Identification of endangered plants and animals, particularly in child's home area		1	2	3	4		
Specific endangered plant and animal species, how some endangerments are being handled, and evaluation of the effects of the applied efforts						5	6
Noise pollution and visual pollution			2	3			
Awareness of costs/benefits of technological and natural solutions to pollution crises			2	3	4	5	6
The history of selected environmental crises; how they were handled, and evaluation of the effects of the applied solution					4	5	6
Limits of science to find solutions to ongoing human/earth environmental problems					4	5	6
Controversies related to current scientific and technological issues					4	5	6
Awareness of environmental protection activities and groups							6

SOCIAL STUDIES

Seven areas are included here: self/family/others, civics/citizenship, government, geography, current events, history, and economics/consumerism. As you can see, we begin this segment where all segments should in theory begin: with the *self*. As in all curricular areas, the youngest learners begin to learn within the realm of what is most familiar to them — themselves, and gradually move concentrically away from themselves. Family is next, neighbors and community follow, and so on, as a gradually expanding process. Historical time is treated similarly — the present time is most understandable to the youngest. The concepts of past and future time come later. In fact, you can approach each area in this manner of gradual expansion. Economics should first involve immediate needs, family economics, local community goods and services. There will be time later for understanding the free enterprise system and still later for understanding international trade. Likewise, citizenship begins with self, family, community, and gradually develops outwards to the concept of international citizenry.

Thus, as you plan the sequence of goals and objectives for your child's social studies curriculum, keep in mind this gradually expanding process of learning that is natural and logical.

Self/Family/Others

Self-awareness (e.g., strengths, abilities, favorite activities, ways child is able to contribute to family life)	K 1 2 3 4 5 6
Sharing important family events/customs	K 1 2 3 4 5 6
Mutual care/support within a family, neighborhood, congregation, community	K 1 2 3 4 5 6
Relationships (e.g., among family, relatives, friends, social groups, community)	K 1 2 3 4 5 6
Informal identification of characteristics that make individual and family lifestyles unique from one another	K 1 2
Economic activities of family members	1 2 3
Family history and origins	3 4 5
Human shelters, similarities and diversity	K 1 2 3
Varying work places and environments	K 1 2 3

Occupations, and the role occupations play in the life of a community	1	2	3		
Awareness of varied ethnic/cultural groups, peoples of other places	1	2	3		
Identifying and characterizing various ethnic groups within one's community and their contributions to the community			3	4		
Identifying various ethnic groups within one's state/nation and their contributions				4	5	6
Comparing and contrasting customs of various ethnic/cultural groups throughout the Western World				4	5	6
Awareness of factors that create cultural changes when people from one culture move into another				4	5	6
Tracing the heritage of selected native and nonnative cultural groups existing in the United States (e.g., Eskimos, Swedish Americans)					5	6
Identifying and characterizing those social/cultural groups who populated and influenced the development of young America during the 1600's; noting their influences on that development					5	6
Exploring human rights issues and groups that influenced those issues during the decades that preceded the Civil War					5	6
Exploring political, occupational, and social groups that have influenced the development of 20th century America					5	6
The advantages and disadvantages of belonging to various kinds of groups			3	4	5	6
Varying roles individuals play in groups			3	4	5	6
The concepts of responsibility, duty, obligation, and individual choice, as they relate to group membership			3	4	5	6
Group decision-making processes			3	4	5	6
Means by which individuals in groups resolve or accept differences			3	4	5	6
Recognizing the influences group members exert upon one another				4	5	6
Awareness of occupational fields related to social studies						6

SOCIAL STUDIES

Civics/Citizenship

	K	1	2	3	4	5	6
Privacy, personal rights, and the effects of one's actions on family and others	K	1	2	3	4	5	6
Respect for the opinions and rights of self, family members, and others	K	1	2	3	4	5	6
Respect for differences in beliefs and values of varied cultures		1	2	3	4	5	6
Why families and communities need rules	K	1	2				
Assisting in the creation of family rules	K	1	2				
Awareness of local community laws and their purposes			2	3			
Ways laws are made and changed				3	4		
Considering the fairness and unfairness of selected rules or laws				3	4		
Awareness of how judicial decisions are made					4	5	6
Awareness of national laws, civil and criminal justice systems, rights of the individual within our system of justice, etc.						5	6
Planning and participating in family, group, and community events	K	1	2	3	4	5	6
Participating in group problem-solving	K	1	2	3	4	5	6
Concept of ownership	K	1	2				
Concept of equal opportunity			2	3	4	5	6
Concept of democracy, constitutional rights, leadership, and voluntary participation			2	3	4	5	6
The role of the citizenry in maintaining a democracy and the importance of individual rights in a democracy such as that of the United States					4	5	6
Significant national and world leaders, and citizens who have "made a difference"					4	5	6
The concept of being a "citizen of the world"						5	6
Discussing what constitutes good vs. bad citizenship in the community, state, nation, and world							6

Government

	K	1	2	3	4	5	6
The term "government"			2	3			
Purposes of local/state/national government			2	3			

Awareness of local, state, and national governmental decisions	2 3			
Services provided through local government	2 3			
Local governmental officials and their functions	2 3			
Local governmental workers and their job-related roles in the community	3 4			
The role of the individual in community problem-solving	3 4			
The right of the individual to form and express his or her own opinion, and to take constructive action with respect to it	3 4 5 6			
State governmental officials, their functions, and other key state leaders	4 5			
The interdependence of a state and its communities	4 5			
The structure and functioning of the branches of state government	4 5 6			
The role of the individual in influencing state social and political issues	4 5 6			
The sources and uses of state monies	4 5			
Services provided through state government	4 5			
The state constitution	4 5			
Elections of governor and of state legislators	4 5			
Interdependence of the nation and states	5 6			
Branches of national government	5 6			
The United States Constitution	5 6			
Means by which individual people express opinions and catalyze change related to national issues	5 6			
The national election process	5 6			
The far-reaching effects of governmental decision-making	5 6			

Geography

Exploration of the earth's surface in the child's home area; features of land and water	K 1 2			
Gathering and recording data about the earth's surface in child's home area	1 2 3			
Observations of living/non-living things in child's home geographical area	K 1 2			

SOCIAL STUDIES

	K	1	2	3	4	5	6
Observations of how people use the earth's surface in child's home area (e.g., farming, manufacturing, recreation)	K	1	2				
How geographical features meet human needs		1	2	3			
Effects of geographical features on people's lives		1	2	3			
Comparing features of land and water in child's home area and elsewhere			2	3	4		
Comparing/contrasting use of the earth's surface in child's area with elsewhere			2	3	4		
Making simple models and maps of a room, a building, and a neighborhood		1	2	3			
Exploration of globes and simple maps		1	2	3			
Distinguishing between land areas and water on globes and maps		1	2	3			
Locating and identifying major geographical regions and their geographical features					4	5	
Comparing and contrasting geographical features region to region					4	5	
Locating communities, counties, states, nations, and continents on maps and globes					4	5	
Studying the geography of child's home state					4	5	
Making models and maps showing the geographic features of child's home state					4	5	
Studying the geography of North, Central, and South America. the Arctic Zone, and Antarctica						5	6
Concept of human migration					4	5	
Regional interaction among peoples					4	5	6
Causes, effects, and history of human migrations, particularly in North, Central, and South America						5	6

Current Events

	K	1	2	3	4	5	6
Means by which people around the world learn about each other daily			2	3	4		
Identifying local current issues, considering solutions, and predicting outcomes			2	3	4	5	6
Noting effects of the past on current events				3	4	5	6

Identifying major state, national, and international current events and issues			3	4	5	6
Focusing on important current issues in child's home state; discussing proposed solutions, designing new solutions, predicting outcomes				4	5	6
Awareness of the role of newspapers as "watchdogs" of key people and institutions involved in the development of current events and issues				4	5	6
Awareness of the potential influence of newspapers on the development of current events and public opinion				4	5	6
Focusing on important national current issues, discussing proposed solutions, designing new solutions, predicting outcomes, identifying key people influencing the issues, considering roles citizens might play in influencing the issues					5	6
Focusing on major international current events and issues and key countries and people involved in those events, discussing proposed solutions, designing new solutions, predicting outcomes						6
The roles of magazines, radio and TV as "watchdogs of key people and institutions involved in the development of current events and issues						6
The potential influence of magazines, radio and TV on the development of current events and public opinion						6

History

Traditional American holidays and their historical backgrounds	K	1	2	3	4	5	6
Objects, words, and lifestyles "of old"	K	1	2	3	4		
Folksongs and other songs of old		1	2	3			
Folklore and other stories of old		1	2	3			
Concept of change in one's own life		1	2	3			
Concept of historical change in one's community, then state, and then nation			2	3			
Focusing on community history and local historical personages			2	3			

SOCIAL STUDIES

Identifying causes of past community change and predicting future change	2 3				
Focusing on state history and state historical personages		4			
Identifying causes of past change within one's own state and predicting future change		4			
Current state historical events; publications		4			
Focusing intermittently on major historical events and people of American history	1 2 3				
Major events in American history, including causes and effects		4 5 6			
Major technological events throughout our historical past		4 5 6			
Evaluating the impact on American society of technological developments of the past		6			
Concepts of rural, urban and suburban; historical change related to these concepts		4 5			
Tracing rural, urban and suburban development, historically, within one's own state, and then the nation		6			
Analyzing and evaluating key decisions that have affected the course of American history; also hypothesize alternative decisions and alternative outcomes		6			

Economics/Consumerism

Basic human needs for food, water, shelter, and clothing and an awareness of community economics related to those needs	K 1 2				
Roles of working family members in acquiring family's basic needs	K 1 2				
Beginning career education		3 4 5 6			
Awareness of uses of money	K 1 2				
Play economics (e.g., games with play money)	1 2				
Real economics, e.g., using money to make purchases, selling goods or services oneself, running a small business	1 2 3				
Personal economic decision-making	2 3 4				
Selling goods or services oneself		3 4 5 6			

Awareness of influences on one's consumer behavior, including advertising methods and techniques				4	5	6	
Developing an awareness of comparison shopping skills				4	5	6	
Energy conservation as an economic measure				4	5	6	
Community workers, stores, goods	K	1	2				
Community services			3	4			
Community economic resources: natural resources, human resources, manmade resources, and their limits or scarcity			3	4			
Goods that are imported to and exported from one's own community			3	4			
Statewide economic resources: natural resources, human resources, manmade resources, and their limits or scarcity				4	5		
The state's economic history				4	5		
The state's manufactured and agricultural products and their importance to the nation and the world				4	5		
Goods that are imported to and exported from one's own state				4	5		
Characteristics of a free enterprise economy and basic elements of America's economic system					5	6	
National economic resources: natural resources, human resources, manmade resources, and their limits or scarcity					5	6	
The nation's manufactured and agricultural products and their importance to the nation and the world					5	6	
Goods that are imported to and exported from the United States					5	6	
Nationwide and worldwide transportation routes and means						6	
Economic resources, and manufactured and agricultural products of Canada and Mexico						6	

MUSIC

Three areas are included here: music appreciation, vocal/instrumental, and listening. In many curriculums, the music segment will not include subheadings, but simply be called *music*. You may elect to use the broader term in your curriculum.

Please remain aware that some children are particularly attuned to musical input and production. In fact, some children's main learning mode is musical. Should this appear to be the case with your child, be sure to infuse all curricular areas with musical activities — at least in daily practice if not in your written curriculum. Letters and numbers, for instance, may be presented musically, along with other presentations. Math may be linked to musical rhythms. Literature may be listened to on records or videos in the form of professional musical productions, as well as actually read. American folksongs and history-related songs may be included in history lessons. Visual art responses to music may be included in art lessons. Physical education lessons, too, may frequently involve music.

Music Appreciation

Listening to a variety of music	K	1	2	3	4	5	6
Physical response to music (e.g., clap, tap) and creative movement inspired by music	K	1	2	3	4	5	6
Recognition of personally pleasing/displeasing music; emotions aroused by music	K	1	2	3	4	5	6
Listening to natural music (e.g., whale songs, bird songs, waves, waterfalls)	K	1	2	3	4	5	6
Recognition of variety and expressiveness created by dynamic contrasts in music				3	4	5	6
Discussion of mood in various musical pieces				3	4	5	6
Music common to earlier time periods		1	2	3	4	5	6
Instruments, styles, moods of music of selected other cultures (e.g., Scottish bagpipes)		1	2	3	4	5	6
Attending live musical performances		1	2	3	4	5	6
Comparing and contrasting recorded and live performances						5	6
Identifying types of songs (e.g., classical, folksong, jazz, country, gospel)						5	6

Major American musicians and composers of today and yesterday					5	6
Participating in organizing and presenting a musical performance					5	6
Awareness of music-related occupations						6

Vocal/Instrumental

	K	1	2	3	4	5	6
Exploration and repetition of rhythms	K	1					
Clapping, tapping, etc., in time to a beat	K	1					
Rhythm patterns as alike and/or different	K	1					
Initiating rhythm patterns for others to echo	K	1					
Singing	K	1					
Playing simple musical instruments	K	1					
Responding to sudden changes in tempo while singing or playing an instrument		1	2	3	4	5	6
Singing with varied instrumental accompaniment		1	2	3	4	5	6
Pitch		1	2	3	4	5	6
Clarity and expressiveness					4	5	6
Playing various musical instruments (percussion, keyboard, and other melodic instruments, and stringed instruments)		1	2	3	4	5	6
Development of a personal song repertoire				3	4	5	6
Playing or singing one part of a two-part song				3	4	5	6
3-part rounds and 2-part harmonizing					4	5	6
American and other nations' folksongs		1	2	3	4	5	6
The state song and national anthem				3	4	5	6
Following standard conducting patterns				3	4	5	6
Terms: refrain, chorus, verse, introduction or coda, melody, solo, quartet, choir, orchestra, band, ensemble, etc.				3	4	5	6
Instrumental improvisation					4	5	6
Playing accompaniments					4	5	6
Identifying common individual musical instruments by sight and by sound			2	3	4	5	6
Identifying individual instruments in combined performances by sound alone						5	6
Identifying soprano, tenor, bass, and alto						5	6
Basic music performance symbols			2	3			
Reading standard rhythmic notations			2	3	4	5	6

MUSIC

	K	1	2	3	4	5	6
Basic understanding of measures and meter signatures (2/4, 3/4, 4/4)			2	3	4		
Differentiating: beat, accent, rhythm pattern				3	4		
Identifying skips, steps, triplets, and repeated notes on a staff				3	4	5	6
Terms: double bar, repeat signs, *fine* and *D.C. al fine, forte, piano, crescendo, diminuendo*				3	4	5	6
Writing simple rhythmic patterns from dictation				3	4		
Writing original rhythmic patterns						5	6
Selecting or composing simple, complete musical pieces; then performing them						5	6
Identifying major, pentatonic scales, and minor, whole tone (six tone) and twelve tone scales						5	6
Identifying the tonal center of a song						5	6
Introduction to sound systems — amplifiers, synthesizers, etc.							6

Listening

	K	1	2	3	4	5	6
Distinguishing between long and short tones, high and low pitches, loud and soft sounds, fast and slow tempos	K	1	2				
Recognizing same or different simple, short melodic patterns	K	1	2				
Experimenting with the sounds and ranges of a variety of available instruments	K	1	2	3	4	5	6
Listening to recorded children's musicals	K	1	2	3	4	5	6
Describing the differentiated qualities of a variety of natural and man-made music		1	2	3	4	5	6
Describing and responding to the moods created by various instruments played during recorded children's musicals			2	3	4	5	6
Identifying musical styles and moods as those of particular cultures and/or of particular musical periods					4	5	6
Developing a sense of musical performance excellence					4	5	6
Developing criteria for critiquing one's own musical performances						5	6

ART

Four areas are included here: basic art tools, art processes and elements of design, color, and art appreciation. While several particular mediums and art methods are noted below, the possibilities are limited only by your ability to teach or to locate someone else who can teach various arts and crafts to your child. In other words, any arts and crafts mediums and methods may be included in your child's curriculum and daily lessons — as long as they are appropriate to your child's interests and ability level.

Basic art tools

Identifying basic tools and mediums by name	K 1 2 3
Care of art tools, equipment, and artwork	K 1 2 3 4 5 6
Using scissors, paints, paintbrushes, glue, paper, palette, easel, and many other art tools to create arts and crafts items	K 1 2 3 4 5 6
Creating crafts with stones, soaps, wood, and other similar mediums	K 1 2 3 4 5 6
Using "found" materials to create crafts	K 1 2 3 4 5 6
Gradually acquiring an understanding and use of art terms: sculpture, photograph, artwork, craft, artist, craftsperson, medium, print, landscape, seascape, portrait, still life, quilting, weaving, border, frame, mobile, statue, poster, stencil, illustration, sketch, water paint, tempera paint, clay, papier-mache, etc.	K 1 2 3 4 5 6
Exploring the role of imagination in art	K 1 2 3 4 5 6

Art Processes and Elements of Design

Exploring colors, shapes, patterns, light and dark, near and far, line, and texture in arts and crafts	K 1 2 3 4 5 6
Exploring contrasts in color, texture, shape	K 1 2 3 4 5 6
Understanding and use of terms: line, drawing, printing, color, shape, texture, figure, subject, design, pattern	K 1 2 3

Describing uses of colors, shapes and repeated patterns in artwork		1 2 3				
Finding a basic shape in an art subject and using the shape to begin a drawing		1 2 3				
Line — diagonal, horizontal, vertical, thick, thin, curved, spiral, concentric		1 2 3				
Terms: foreground, background		1 2 3				
Using perspective in art projects			3 4 5 6			
Building basic three dimensional shapes: box, cone, cylinder			3 4 5 6			
Creating patterns and designs for aesthetic effects using three dimensional shapes			3 4 5 6			
Exploring action and movement in three dimensional forms			3 4 5 6			
Creating varied textures, implied or real		1 2 3				
Concept of "center of interest"		1 2 3				
Uses of and problems with space in artwork		1 2 3				
Drawing, water painting, block printing		1 2 3				
Collages, murals, carving and sculpture		2 3 4 5 6				
Braiding, weaving and other textile arts		2 3 4 5 6				
Batik, stitchery, applique			5 6			
Jewelry making, profile drawing, calligraphy			5 6			
Creating varied art with a consciousness of medium, mode, mood, and depth			3 4 5 6			
Gradual inclusion of greater detail in artwork			3 4 5 6			
Artistic decision-making: patterns, colors, subjects, themes, media, shapes, etc.			3 4 5 6			
Artistic planning and problem solving: an entire art project from first inspiration to gathering information, materials; planning; evaluating in-progress; solving in-progress problems, completing the piece			5 6			
Critiquing one's own art-in-progress			5 6			

Color

Identification of primary and secondary colors and of black and white	K 1 2 3					
Recognizing and enjoying colors in nature	K 1 2 3					
Using colors in the creation of arts projects	K 1 2 3 4 5 6					
Turning primary colors into secondary colors	1 2 3					

ART

Mixing black and white with primary and secondary colors		1	2	3		
Identifying complementary colors		1	2	3		
Terms: value, shade, tint, warm, cool, neutral				3	4 5 6
The effects of side-by-side lights and darks and side-by-side colors of similar value				3	4 5 6
Uses of color to create emphasis and mood					4 5 6

Art Appreciation

Displaying artwork of self and other children	K	1	2	3	4	5	6
Explaining one's own art and art processes	K	1	2	3	4	5	6
Discussing pleasing effects of colors, shapes, patterns, and designs in nature	K	1	2	3	4	5	6
Identifying alike and different subjects and moods in art	K	1	2	3	4	5	6
Awareness of realism and the abstract in art			2	3	4	5	6
Awareness of design symmetry/asymmetry			2	3	4	5	6
Awareness of community art activities			2	3	4	5	6
Awareness of state/national art activities					4	5	6
Noting similarities in art of one culture				3	4	5	6
Examples of art from past time periods				3	4	5	6
Introduction to art history						5	6
Locating major galleries in one's own state					4	5	
Locating major galleries in the United States						5	6
Identification of particular artists by viewing their art				3	4	5	6
Exploring personalities of artists and how they are reflected in art					4	5	6
Learning about major artists within the child's home state and about their art					4	5	
Identifying major American artists by viewing their art						5	6
Understanding and respecting the value of great art						5	6
Awareness of art as an occupational field							6

PHYSICAL EDUCATION

Four areas are included here: body awareness and control, physical fitness, recreation, health and safety. The single heading *physical education* may be used, or two headings, *physical education* and *health.*

Body Awareness and Control

Exploration of patterns of movement (e.g., walking, running, hopping, skipping, jumping, leaping, galloping, sliding)	K	1	2				
Exploration of speed, direction, and space	K	1	2				
Exploration of body configuration (e.g., sway, bend, stretch, twist, sit, stand, lie down)	K	1	2				
Exploration of strength (e.g., push, pull, hold)	K	1	2				
Manipulation of small objects, eye-hand control (e.g., stringing beads, writing)	K	1	2				
Physical response to music, including dance	K	1	2	3	4	5	6
Directional response (e.g., forward, backward, over, up, down, under, left, right, through, around, inside, outside)	K	1	2				
Posture	K	1	2	3	4	5	6
Simple tumbling (e.g., forward roll, balancing)	K	1	2				
Jumping rope		1	2	3	4		
Body-object control (e.g., catch, throw, kick)		1	2	3	4		
Throwing and kicking objects to a target		1	2	3	4		
Striking a ball backhand, forehand, underhand, overhand, and with both hands		1	2	3	4		
Striking a ball with a bat, mallet, paddle, etc.			2	3	4	5	6
Balancing on a balance beam			2	3	4	5	6
Swimming and swimming survival			2	3	4	5	6
Flowing, smooth physical movement			2	3	4	5	6
Simple gymnastics			2	3	4	5	6

Physical Fitness

	K	1	2	3	4	5	6
Discussion of feelings of energy and tiredness, strength and weakness	K	1	2				
Leisure time physical activities	K	1	2	3	4	5	6
Relationship of physical fitness to health	K	1	2				
The beneficial effects of fresh air and exercise	K	1	2				
Light stretching/flexibility exercises			2	3	4	5	6
Light aerobic exercises (e.g., distance walking, light dance-exercise, swimming)			2	3	4	5	6
Endurance (e.g., gradual conditioning for distance walking and jogging)					4	5	6
Light strength exercises					4	5	6
Balancing sedentary with physical activity and indoor with outdoor activity	K	1	2	3	4	5	6
Observation of adults, including senior citizens, engaging in "life-sports"					4	5	6
Development of the habit of fitness activities					4	5	6

Recreation

	K	1	2	3	4	5	6
Cooperation in play	K	1	2	3	4	5	6
Game rules, procedures, and play	K	1	2	3	4	5	6
Equipment and equipment care	K	1	2	3	4	5	5
More complex individual and teamwork activities (e.g., juggling, golf, soccer)				3	4	5	6
Sportsmanship and self-acceptance				3	4	5	6
Dance (e.g., explorative, improvisational, American folk, traditional ethnic dance)	K	1	2	3	4	5	6
Physical activities involving discovery/problem-solving (e.g., treasure hunt, reaching heights, maneuvering in low spaces)	K	1	2	3	4	5	6
Fitness activities as recreation	K	1	2	3	4	5	6
Affective benefits of recreation				3	4	5	6
Making a habit of physical recreation				3	4	5	6
Seeking leisure time physical activities with self confidence, enthusiasm, and a sense of one's own physical abilities				3	4	5	6
Awareness of physical recreation participated in by many in our society					4	5	6
Discussion of and practice of leadership, mutual encouragement, and acceptable aggressiveness in team games						5	6

PHYSICAL EDUCATION

Health and Safety

	K	1	2	3	4	5	6
Concept of safety	K	1	2				
Responsibility for personal safety	K	1	2	3			
Emergency readiness/response (e.g., 911)	K	1	2	3			
Basic safety measures (e.g., fire safety)	K	1	2	3			
Basic symptoms of ailments or illness to report to adults (e.g., sore throat, cuts)	K	1	2	3			
Basic health measures (e.g., cleanliness)	K	1	2	3			
Health/safety-related rights of self and others		1	2	3	4		
Identifying external body parts	K	1	2	3			
Sensory functions of nose, ears, eyes, mouth	K	1	2	3			
Awareness of eye and ear health measures		1	2	3			
Knowledge of basic health products		1	2	3			
Awareness of tooth decay and causes		1	2	3			
Common poisons		1	2	3			
Knowledge of appropriate clothing in relationship to weather conditions		1	2	3			
The individuality of growth and appearance		1	2	3			
The beneficial effects of rest and sleep	K	1	2	3			
The importance of water consumption	K	1	2	3			
The beneficial effects of physical exercise	K	1	2	3			
The beneficial effects of humor and laughter		1	2	3			
Communicable vs. noncommunicable diseases and discussing their prevention		1	2	3			
The relationship of heredity to diseases					4	5	6
Familiarization with health workers		1	2	3			
Basic nutritional needs			2	3	4		
Consciousness of *choice* as a determiner of good personal health practices			2	3	4		
Specific emotions, causes and effects	K	1	2	3	4	5	6
Dealing with emotions	K	1	2	3	4	5	6
The support role family and friends play in one's mental and physical health			2	3	4	5	6
Recreation safety			2	3	4	5	6
Basic drug awareness facts						5	6
Environmental health issues						5	6
Animal reproduction							6

Appendix B

RESOURCES

Finding Categories of Goals and Objectives

As noted in Chapter 4, you may find ideas for categories of goals and objectives to include in your curriculum from six sources: sample curriculums, sample grade level textbooks, subject-related books written by experts, an experienced teacher of the subject, an expert in the field, or the "K-6 Subject Area Breakdown" provided in this book. There are, in addition, a few resources which either outline subject area goals and objectives, outline the categories more generally, or discuss a subject thoroughly enough for you to derive goals and objectives from them. A few such resources are listed below.

Many of these resources will be available in libraries, particularly college libraries. Don't be shy about asking a librarian for assistance in locating books on teaching specific subject areas, books related to curricula, sample textbooks, and reference books. Remember, too, that in college libraries you are likely to find several books not listed here that will provide complete K-6, K-12, and/or 7-12 curriculum outlines which can be used as samples. You might also discover some of the resources listed below in the hands of fellow home schoolers or in a support group lending collection. You'll see that with the one-time purchase of some of the books listed below, you could have all you'll ever need for an entire K-3, K-6, or K-12 curriculum in the treated subject area.

[NOTE: Such designations as *K-3* denote grade levels; *pre* refers to preschool.]

"Barbe Reading Skills Check List." Prentice-Hall, Prentice-Hall Bldg., 113 Sylvan Ave., Englewood Cliffs NJ 07632. (K-6 reading skills listed by grade level. Useful for developing a reading curriculum and for designing ongoing assessments of student progress.)

Barrata-Lorton, Mary. *Math Their Way*, 1976. Addison-Wesley, One Jacob Way, Redding MA 01867. (A manipulative, activity-centered math program for pre-K-2 from which a partial math curriculum could be derived. Addison-Wesley supplies other math texts and materials as well.)

Bauer, Marion Dane. *What's Your Story? A Young Person's Guide to Writing Fiction*, 1992. Clarion Books, 215 Park Ave. South, New York NY 10003. (Step-by-step guide to writing short stories that lends itself to grades 7-12 curriculum development in this area.)

Beechick, Ruth. *The Three R's Series—K-3*, 1986. Arrow Press, P.O. Box 899, Pollock Pines CA 95726. (Manuals listing expectations for each grade with ideas for teaching reading, language, and math.)

Beechick, Ruth. *You Can Teach Your Child Successfully: Grades 4-8*, 1992. Arrow Press, P.O. Box 899, Pollock Pines CA 95726. (Curriculum ideas.)

Brown, Tom, Jr. and Judy Brown. *Tom Brown's Field Guide to Nature and Survival for Children*, 1989. Berkley Publishing, 200 Madison Ave., New York NY 10016. (Curricular items on identifying animals/plants, stalking/tracking, finding water and food in the wilderness, and safety.)

Copperman, Paul. *Taking Books to Heart; How to Develop a Love of Reading in Your Child*, 1986. Addison-Wesley, One Jacob Way, Redding MA 01867. (Explanations of basal readers—reading textbooks—for children ages 2-9, beginning reading and comprehension instruction, and descriptions of at-home reading sessions. Includes activities and book lists.)

Earle, Richard A. *Teaching Reading and Mathematics*, 1976. International Reading Asso., P.O. Box 8139, Newark DE 19711. (On the process of reading necessary for mathematics, such as reading word problems. Useful for planning a math curriculum, particularly above grade 3.

Elbow, Peter. *Writing Without Teachers*, 1973. Oxford University Press, Inc., 200 Madison Ave., New York NY 10016. (On teaching the writing process. From this book you may derive a writing curriculum based upon the writing process. Also includes a small list of reference books and textbooks useful with a home writing curriculum.)

Graves, Donald. *Writing: Teachers and Children at Work*, 1989. Heinemann, 36 Hanover St., Portsmouth NH 03801. (On developing a process oriented writing curriculum.)

Graves, Donald and Virginia Stuart. *Write From the Start: Tapping Your Child's Natural Writing Abilities*, 1987. Dutton, 375 Hudson St., New York NY 10014-3657. (Writing curriculum ideas.)

Groff, Patrick and Dorothy Z. Seymour. *Word Recognition; the Why and the How*, 1987. Charles C. Thomas Publishing, 2600 S. First St., Springfield IL 62717. (How to teach beginning reading, particularly phonics. Could form the basis of a reading curriculum.)

Hirsch, E.D., Jr. *The Core Knowledge Series*. Doubleday Consumer Services, P. O. Box 5071, Des Plaines IL 60017-5071 (Grade-level literacy guides.)

Hirsch, E.D., Jr. *Cultural Literacy; What Every American Needs to Know*, 1989, and *A First Dictionary of Cultural Literacy: What Our Children Need to Know*, 1989. Houghton Mifflin Co., 222 Berkeley St., Boston MA 02107. (On what American students ought to be learning.)

Hoffman, Jane. *The Backyard Scientist*, Series I, II, III, IV, 1987, 1989, 1990, 1992. Backyard Scientist, P.O. Box 16966, Irvine CA 92713. (Science activities upon which one could partially base a science curriculum.)

Hull, Marion A. *Phonics for the Teacher of Reading; Programmed for Self-Instruction*, 1993. Merrill Publishing Co., P.O. Box 508, Columbus OH 43216. (A self-instructional text useful for home-teachers planning a phonics curriculum and who want to learn phonics well themselves.)

Kaufman, Felice. *Your Gifted Child and You*, 1983. Council for Exceptional Children, Dept. CS88M, 1920 Association Dr., Reston VA 22091-1589. (On helping gifted children develop their interests, with thought-stimulators particular to developing a curriculum for gifted/talented children.)

Koch, Kenneth. *Rose, where did you get that red? Teaching Great Poetry to Children*, 1990. Random House, 201 E. Fiftieth St., New York NY 10022. (Descriptions of how to teach poetry to children. The poetry segment of a K-6 literature/reading curriculum could be derived from this book.)

Larrick, Nancy *A Parent's Guide to Children's Reading*, 1983. Doubleday, Doubleday Consumer Services, P.O. Box 5071, Des Plaines IL 60017-5071. (On the teaching of reading.)

Levine, Harold. *Vocabulary for the College-Bound*. Amsco School Publications, Inc., 315 Hudson St., New York NY 10013. (Text upon which the vocabulary portion of a 9-12 English curriculum could be based.)

Lipson, Eden Ross. *The New York Times Parent's Guide to Best Books for Children*, 1991. Times Books, 201 East 50th St., New York NY 10022. (A pre-K-12 best-books bibliography.)

Moffett, James. *Active Voice: A Writing Program Across the Curriculum*, 1992. Boynton Cook, 361 Hanover St., Portsmouth NH 03801.

Moffett, James and Betty Jane Wagner. *Student-Centered Language Arts and Reading, K-13: A Handbook for Teachers*, 1991. Houghton Mifflin, 222 Berkeley St., Boston MA 02108. (K-13 language/reading curriculum.)

National Science Teacher Association. *Recommended Model for Developing a K-12 Science Skills Continuum*, 1982. Nat'l Science Teachers Asso., 1840 Wilson Blvd., Arlington VA 22201 (K-12 science curriculum.)

Naturescope. Nat'l Wildlife Federation, 8925 Leesburg Pike, Vienna VA 22184. (A series of teaching guides for nature-science education—useful for designing segments of and teaching a home-school nature-science curriculum. Ask for a catalog of all available issues.)

Orlick, Terry. *The Cooperative Sports and Games Book* and *The Second Cooperative Sports and Games Book*. Pantheon, 201 E. 50th St., New York NY 10022. (Useful for developing the recreational segment of a physical education curriculum. Also related to citizenship and socialization skills.)

Pollock, Marion B. and Kathleen Middleton. *Elementary School Health Instruction*, 1989. Mosby College Publishing, 11830 Westline Industrial Dr., St. Louis MO 63146. (K-6 health curriculum rosters which could be helpful in constructing a full K-6 health curriculum for about $30.)

"Reading Beyond the Basals," Perfection Form Co., 1000 N. Second Ave., Logan IA 51546. (A series of booklets upon which one could derive portions of a literature curriculum for elementary children. Full of reading comprehension activities to accompany selected children's books.)

Reuther, Barbara McNally and Diane Enemark Fogler. *Primary Level Art Curriculum Activities Kit: Primary Level*; also *Intermediate Level*, 1988. Parker Publishing, West Nyack NY 10995. (Provides 75 easy-to-use lessons exploring 8 different media to teach art concepts/skills, grades 1-4. A 4-year home art curriculum could be derived from this one book.)

Smookler, Norvin. *The Reader's Art; Concepts and Terms in Literature*, 1972. Holt, Rinehart and Winston, Inc., 6277 Sea Harbor Dr., Orlando FL 32887. (Discussions of common elements of literature with examples. Useful for developing a literature curriculum, 9-12.)

Spalding, Romalda Bishop and Walter T. Spalding. *The Writing Road to Reading*, 1990. Quill, 1350 Avenue of the Americas, New York NY 10019. (An easy-to-use program for teaching phonics and beginning spelling and reading—from which one could derive a curriculum for these subjects.)

Spiegel, Dixie Lee. *Reading for Pleasure: Guidelines*, 1984. International Reading Association, P.O. Box 8139, Newark DE 19711. (On developing a reading program which encourages recreational reading. Useful both for planning the recreational reading portion of a reading curriculum and setting up a home library.)

Stanford, Gene. *Steps to Better Writing; a Systematic Approach to Expository Writing*, 1972. Holt, Rinehart and Winston, 6277 Sea Harbor Dr., Orlando FL 32887. (An easy-to-use text for basic junior high or early high school expository writing which could become the basis of that portion of a writing curriculum which covers expository writing.)

Stenmark, Jean Kerr, et. al. *Family Math*. Family Math, 1986. Lawrence Hall of Science, Univ. of California, Berkeley CA 94720. (A book full of hands-on math activities and rosters of typical grade-level math curricula.)

Stribling, Mary Lou. *Art from Found Materials*, 1970. Crown, 201 E. 50th St., New York NY 10022. (Inexpensive art projects from which an art curriculum based upon varied mediums could be derived, grade 3 and up.

Swan, Malcolm D., editor. *Tips and Tricks in Outdoor Education, 1994.*. Interstate Printers and Publishers, Inc., P.O. Box 50, Danville IL 61834. (Activities and plans for learning in the out-of-doors. Especially useful in developing science curricula, but also for social studies curricula, environmental awareness, and nature arts and crafts.)

Thomas, Jerry R., et. al. *Physical Education for Children; Daily Lesson Plans*, 1989. Human Kinetics Books, Box 5076, Champaign IL 61820. (Entire K-6 physical education curriculum and planned lessons—at the cost of about $35 for this king-size, 3-ring binder from which a complete home PE curriculum could be derived.)

Ward, Ann. *Learning at Home*, 1988. Noble Publishing, P.O. Box 2250, Gresham OR 97030. (Day-by-day preschool and kindergarten lesson plans. Also, first grade and second grade guides. Each in the $40 range.)

Finding Texts and Materials

You will find many resources noted in various home-school books and magazines. Some of references below simply list textbooks and teaching materials, while others offer annotations or reviews. In lieu of textbooks, some list subject-related books which could effectively substitute for traditional textbooks or become part of a home library. Finally, many listed below are themselves resources.

Anthro Notes. ATTN: P.A. Kaupp, Anthropology Outreach and Public Info. Office, Dept. of Anthropology, NHB 363 MRC 112, Smithsonian Institution, Washington DC 20560. (A bulletin for teachers with subject-specific articles, activities, teaching ideas, and recommended books. Published three times a year by the Nat'l Museum of Natural History.)

Armstrong, Thomas. *In Their Own Way; Discovering and Encouraging Your Child's Personal Learning Style*, 1988. J.T. Tarcher Inc., 5858 Wilshire Blvd., Suite 200, Los Angeles CA 90036. (Explanations of learning styles and teaching techniques adapted to those styles. Lists of references and organizations which may lead to texts, materials, and other help.)

Arts & Activities. Suite 200, 591 Camino de la Reina, San Diego CA 92108. (Learning activities magazine for art education, materials and publications reviews, clip-and-save art prints.)

Cobblestone. 7 School Street, Peterborough NH 03458. (Grades 4-9 children's magazine focusing on American history with firsthand accounts, lively biographies, poems, maps, games, puzzles, cartoons, songs, recipes, contests, resource lists, historic photos and illustrations.)

Colfax, David and Micki Colfax. *Homeschooling for Excellence*, 1988. Mountain House Press, Box 353, Philo CA 95466. (A book about home schooling in general, but includes notations of texts, reference books, and other books useful to home-school families.)

"Consumer Information Catalog." Consumer Information Catalog, P.O. Box 100, Pueblo CO 81009. (Lists free and low-cost publications on various subjects including consumer education.)

DeVito, Alfred and Gerald H. Krockover. *Creative Sciencing; Ideas and Activities for Teachers and Children, Grades K-8*, 1991. Little, Brown and Co., 200 West Street, Waltham MA 02154. (Science resources.)

Duffy, Cathy. *Christian Home Educator's Curriculum Manual-Elementary Grades*, 1992. Home Run Enterprises, 12531 Aristocrat Avenue, Garden Grove CA 92641. (Guide to establishing a Christian home curriculum, including many materials recommendations.)

Duffy, Cathy. *Christian Home Educator's Curriculum Manual-Junior/Senior High*, 1992. Home Run Enterprises. (Guide to a junior/senior high level, Christian home curriculum.)

Growing Without Schooling. Holt Associates, 2269 Massachusetts Ave., Cambridge MA 02140. (A bimonthly magazine including informative letters from readers, articles, texts and materials information, and more.)

Hegener, Mark and Helen Hegener, editors. *The Home School Reader*, 1988. Home Education Press, P.O. Box 1083, Tonasket WA 98855. (Anthology of articles about home schooling, including a few about curriculum development and with notations of useful texts and materials.)

Hendrickson, Borg. *Home School: Taking the First Step*, 1994. Mountain Meadow Press, P.O. Box 318, Sitka AK 99835. (Guide to all aspects of home schooling; questions/answers, curriculum, record keeping, complete resource lists, curriculum/texts/ materials suppliers. An appendix which explains general teaching approaches and those particular to the teaching of reading, and an excellent glossary of educational terms..)

Home Education Magazine. Home Education Press, P.O. Box 1083, Tonasket WA 98855. (Magazine offering activity pages for children, book and materials reviews, and helpful articles on methods of teaching at home.)

Homefires. 180 El Camino Real, Suite 10, Millbrae CA 94030. (Publication including resources and educational events, directory, historical/biographical calendar, family adventures, multicultural events, and pages for and by children (stories, poems, art, math/science/craft activities.)

Hubbs, Don. *Home Education Resource Guide*, 1994. Blue Bird Publishing, 1713 E. Broadway #306, Tempe AZ 85282. (A directory of home-education resource materials.)

National Science Resources Center. *Science for Children; Resources for Teachers*, 1988. National Academy Press, 2101 Constitution Ave. NW, Lockbox 285, Washington DC 20418. (A book full of resources — curriculum materials, supplementary resources, and non-book sources of information and assistance; with two grade-level indexes.)

"Notable 1995 Children's Trade Books in the Field of Social Studies." CBC, 568 Broadway, Suite 404, New York NY 10012. (An annual list of some of the best books for children that cover social studies subjects.)

"Outstanding Science Trade Books for Children in 1995." CBC, 568 Broadway, Suite 404, New York NY 10012. (An annual list of some of the best books for children that cover science subjects.)

Pride, Bill and Mary Pride. *Pride's Guide to Educational Software.*, 1992 Crossway Books, 1300 Crescent Street, Wheaton IL 60187. (Reviews over 750 software programs, pre-K-12, all subjects.)

Pride, Mary. *The Big Books of Home Learning*, Volumes 1, 2, 3, 4. Great Christian Books, 1319 Newport Gap Pike, Wilmington DE 19804. (Large directories of home-education resource materials.)

The Reading Edge. P.O. Box 3, Crownsville MD 21032. (Reviews of current children's books to facilitate selection by parents.)

Reed, Arthea. *Comics to Classics: A Parent's Guide to Books for Teens and Preteens,* 1994. Penguin Books, 375 Hudson Street, New York NY 10014-3657.

Reed, Donn. *The Home School Source Book,* 1991. Brook Farm Books, P.O. Box 246, Bridgewater ME 04735. (Catalog and directory of home-school learning materials and supplies.)

Resources for the Gifted. Resources for the Gifted, 3421 N. 44th St., Phoenix AZ 85018.

Rowell, Elizabeth H. and Thomas B. Goodkind. *Teaching the Pleasures of Reading,* 1982. Prentice-Hall, Inc., Prentice-Hall Bldg., 113 Sylvan Avenue, Rte 9W, Englewood Cliffs NJ 07632. (Activities/readings/materials lists for the teaching of reading.)

Rupp, Rebecca. *Good Stuff: Learning Tools for All Ages,* 1994. Home Education Press, P.O. Box 1083, Tonasket WA 98855. (Resource guide covering most subject areas and children's literature.)

Saul, Wendy and Alan R. Newman. *Science Fare: An Illustrated Guide and Catalog of Toys, Books, and Activities for Kids,* 1986. HarperCollins, 10 E. 53rd Street, New York, NY 10022-5299.

Simic, Marjorie R. and others. *The Curious Learner: Help Your Child Develop Academic and Creative Skills,* 1992. Grayson-Bernard, P.O. Box 5247, Bloomington IN 47407. (On encouraging curiosity and enthusiasm in learners. Includes subject-related resources.)

Softworlds for Children. P.O. Box 219, Edmonds WA 98020. (A buyer's guide which reviews MacIntosh computer software for children.)

Stillman, Peter R. *Families Writing,* 1992. Writer's Digest Books, 1507 Dana Ave., Cincinnati OH 45207. (Full of family-style writing activities. Includes a list of related books for students of writing.)

Teaching Exceptional Children. Council on Exceptional Children, 1920 Association Dr., Reston VA 22091-1589. (Magazine with practical instructional methods, materials, and techniques for working with children who have disabilities or who are gifted.

The Teaching Home. P.O. Box 20219, Portland OR 97220-0219. (Magazine covering many Christian home-school topics, resource and materials descriptions, and articles on teaching methods.)

Trelease, Jim. *The Read-Aloud Handbook,* 1985. Penguin Books, 375 Hudson St., New York, NY 10014. (Discussion of elements of a reading program, methods of teaching reading, and a guide to more than 300 read-aloud children's books.)

Williams, Jane. *How to Stock a Quality Home Library Inexpensively.,* 1994 Bluestocking Press, P.O. Box 1014, Placerville CA 95667.

Williams, Jane. *Young Thinkers Bookshelf: Books to Encourage Independent and Critical Thinking*, 1989. Bluestocking Press, P.O. Box 1014, Placerville CA 95667. (On book selection for a graduated reading program, indexed by subjects. 300 books to stimulate creative and intuitive thought, reasoning skills, self-directed growth, and character development.)

Williams, Jane. *Who Reads What When: Literature Selections for Children Ages Three Through Thirteen*. Bluestocking Press, P.O. Box 1014, Placerville CA 95667. (Lists over 500 children's books, indexed by age, author, and title.)

WonderScience.. American Chemical Society, 1155 16th St. NW, Washington DC 20036. (Magazine of hands-on physical science experiments, activities, and information for parents to use with elementary age students.

Young Children. (National Association for the Education of Young Children, 1509 16th St. NW, Washington DC 10036-1426. (Magazine with informational articles and teaching ideas for teachers of pre-K-3.)

Building a Basic Reference Book Library

Your reference library may begin quite inexpensively and simply. If your child is a primary student, you may wish to concentrate on building a good children's book library before purchasing any of what we commonly call "reference books." By first or second grade you might add an elementary dictionary and atlas. By third grade perhaps a children's thesaurus and an English usage handbook (for use by you as well as your child). An encyclopedia set is nice to have close-at-hand by third grade, too, but is not by any means essential if you live within driving distance of a library or if you have a computer with a CD ROM player for which you could by an enclyclopedia on a CD for less than $100.00. Encyclopedia *book* sets are often prohibitively expensive and, as librarians well know, will be out-of-date in about five years. If you are determined, however, to buy one, you may want to wait until your child is most likely to use the set often — junior high or high school age — so that the encyclopedia set remains up-to-date for your child's remaining home-school years. Keep in mind, too, that many reference books are regularly revised and updated, sometimes annually, so when locating any listed below, be sure to ask for the edition published in the noted year or the latest edition.

There are literally hundreds of reference books, beyond a basic collection — geographical and biographical dictionaries, outdoor field guides, contemporary English usage guides, bibliographies, indexes, anthologies, and on and on. Your child's interests and curriculum will lead you to some of them, but most are available in libraries everywhere, so that few will need to be purchased.

Those references listed below comprise a basic list from which to begin your search for those you'd like to purchase for your home reference library.

Anthony, Susan C. *Facts Plus: An Almanac of Essential Information,* 1992. Instructional Resources Co., Dimond Blvd., #188, Anchorage AK 99515-2099. (A book covering basic facts, concepts, statistics, etc., in most subject areas. Also. *Facts Plus Activity Book,* a teacher's guide to activities that help kids learn to use reference books.)

Arbuthnot, May Hill. *The Arbuthnot Anthology of Children's Literature,* 1976. Scott, Foresman & Co., 1900 E. Lake Ave., Glenview IL 60025. (A comprehensive collection of tales and poetry.)

The Cambridge Annotated Study Bible, 1993. Cambridge University Press, 40 W. 20th St., New York NY 10011-4211. (Includes study notes, concordance, tables of chronology and measures, and parallel gospels.)

Grisewood, John. The Kingfisher Illustrated Children's Dictionary, 1994. Kingfisher LKC, 95 Madison Ave., New York NY 10016. (Grades 5 and up.)

Grisewood, John. *Simon and Schuster's Illustrated Young Readers Dictionary,* 1984. Simon and Schuster, Rockefeller Center, 1230 Avenue of the Americas, New York NY 10029. (Nicely illustrated, clear definitions with many sample sentences to show uses of words.)

Jerome, Judson. *Poet's Handbook,* 1986. Writer's Digest Books, 1507 Dana Ave., Cincinnati OH 45207. (Explanations and samples of the elements of poetry, useful as a reference for literature lessons.)

Koch, Kenneth and Kate Farrell. *Talking to the Sun: An Illustrated Anthology of Poems for Young People,* 1985. H. Holt, 115 W. 18th St., New York NY 10011.

The New American Roget's College Thesaurus in Dictionary Form, 1994. NAL-Dutton, 375 Hudson St., New York NY 10014-3657. (An easy-to-use dictionary of synonyms, useful as a reference for 7-12 writing lessons.)

The New International Atlas., 1994. Rand McNally, 8255 N. Central Pk., Skokie IL 60076-2970. (A comprehensive atlas useful as a social studies reference book for grades 4-12.)

O'Mahony, Kieran. *The Dictionary of Geographical Literacy: The Complete Geography Reference,* 1993. EduCare Press, P. O. Box 31511, Seattle WA 98103. (Dictionary of geographical concepts, ideas, and places.)

The Random House Atlas of the Oceans, 1991. Random House, 201 E. 50th St., New York NY 10022.

The Random House College Dictionary. Random House, Inc., 201 E. 50th St., New York NY 10022. (Grades 9-12.)

Russell, William F. *Classics to Read Aloud to Your Children,* 1992. Crown, 201 E. 50th S., New York NY 10003. (Classic literature excerpts.)

Sabin, William A. *The Gregg Reference Manual,* 1985. McGraw-Hill Book Co., 1221 Avenue of the Americas, New York NY 10020. (Comprehensive quick-reference guide to English usage—grammar, punctuation, capitalization, etc. Useful during writing and language lessons.)

The Teen Study Bible, New International Version, 1993. Zondervan, 5300 Patterson Ave. SE, Grand Rapids MI 49530. (For ages 12-16.)

Williams, Joseph M. *Style; Toward Clarity and Grace,* 1990. University of Chicago Press, 5801 Ellis Ave., 4th Floor, Chicago IL 60637. (A text and reference book for the college-bound composition student.)

Wittels, Harriet and Joan Greisman. *The Clear and Simple Thesaurus Dictionary.* Grosset and Dunlap, 200 Madison Ave., New York NY 10016. (A dictionary of synonyms for elementary level home students, for use with their writing curriculum.)

The Word in Life Study Bible, 1993. Thomas Nelson, Nelson Place at Elm Hill Pike, Nashville TN 37214. (Includes fact boxes, maps, and study notes.)

GLOSSARY

ability level The maximum level at which a child is able to perform successfully, due to intelligence and previous learning.

academic progress The movement by a child through a sequence of learning objectives in a curriculum as demonstrated by mastery of the skills and concepts involved.

achievement Mastery of learned skills and knowledge.

administrator A person who administers a school or school district, or has a particular administrative responsibility within either, such as a superintendent, a principal, or director of special education.

age/grade appropriateness A curriculum which is age/grade appropriate includes learning goals and objectives that a student will typically master at a particular age/grade based upon normal intellectual, emotional and physical development. Example: Children normally do not fully understand the concept of cause and effect until they are beyond the ages of primary students; likewise with the development of sufficient hand-eye coordination to write within narrow lines. What constitutes "normal" in the case of age/grade appropriate curriculum may not be normal for your child or dozens of other children, but, nevertheless, age/grade appropriateness is often expected in home-school curriculums.

ancillary services, public school Services which may be available at a public school beyond regular classroom instruction, such as the services of a physical therapist, a special education instructor, a hearing or speech specialist, an instructor of the blind.

art education Instruction in and practice with colors, depth perception, shapes, size relationships, picture composition, art mediums, art appreciation and history, and so on.

assessment An evaluation of a student's progress or achievement in a particular educational subject, program or setting. Such an assessment may include formal tests, quizzes, oral testing, review of past work, observations and/or interviews, and other means of evaluation.

basic skills Core courses or subjects taught in a school, such as reading, language, math, social studies, and science; and basic or common skills within those core subjects, such as addition, subtraction, division, and multiplication in math.

business education Instruction in the skills associated with office work, such as typing, shorthand, business English, office machines, bookkeeping, accounting, marketing, computers in business, and additional business-related courses. Business education courses may come under the umbrella of "vocational education." At home school, experiential entrepreneurship may be a vehicle for business education.

career education Instruction about the world of work that typically includes job categories, training requirements, salaries and working conditions, career paths, and the choices involved in career decision-making.

certified supervisor A state-certified teacher who assists a home-school parent in various aspects of the home-schooling process, such as planning a curriculum. Working with a certified consultant or supervisor may be required by a state's home-school statutes and regulations.

citizenship The inculcation of particular societal values in children, such as learning to be considerate of other children, to play cooperatively, to contribute to group efforts, to develop a sense of one's role in American society and the roles of others, and so on.

communications A course in the language arts. May specifically refer to oral communications or a speech course. [*see also* language arts]

compulsory attendance laws The legal requirement in all states that children of certain ages be enrolled in a school or other education program.

computer literacy The ability to understand basic computer terminology and to utilize a computer in performing rudimentary tasks, such as simple word processing.

consumer education Instruction in the skills and knowledge necessary to be an informed consumer in our economic system. Examples include critical analysis of advertising, understanding consumer credit, and savings and investment alternatives.

core curriculum The basic subjects, including reading, language arts and math, and in most cases also science and social studies.

cumulative curriculum [*see* curriculum]

cumulative permanent record A record of a child's educational progress maintained throughout a child's school years. This file includes yearly grades in all courses, attendance records, and achievement test scores. A copy of a child's permanent record is normally transferred with the child from school to school.

curriculum The content of an instructional program; i.e., what a student is to be taught and/or is to learn. Usually a curriculum appears in roster or outline form, including broad learning goals and specific learning objectives, and is often prefaced by educational philosophies and long-term educational aims. The curriculum is arranged in what is termed sequential (cumulative, progressive, or sustained) order; that is, from least advanced to most advanced skill levels. [*see also* core curriculum]

curriculum guide A book or notebook containing a curriculum. [*see also* curriculum]

curriculum mastery The development by a student of a high degree of competence in the skills delineated in a given curriculum and of an understanding of the content of that curriculum which transcends rote learning of facts.

department of education The branch of state government that licenses teachers, disburses state funds to school districts, administers federal education programs within a state, and oversees the implementation of state laws governing education.

documentation A written record generally considered as proof to an authority. In the case of home schooling, such items as an attendance register, curriculum outlines, teacher's lesson plan book and/or daily log, and test results — any or all of which may constitute proof that a parent is teaching a sound curriculum and is meeting state statutes regulating home instruction.

emotionally-disturbed child A child whose state of emotional health requires that he be given special instruction or other services to enable him to achieve an acceptable level of academic progress.

equivalent instruction A term included in several states' home-schooling statutes to indicate that a home-school curriculum must be closely correlated with the public school curriculum in the local district or state. However, the exact meaning of *equivalent instruction* in any one state may be subject to interpretive review during home-school litigation.

evaluation of students Testing or other observational data-gathering that enables a teacher or other school personnel to determine a child's learning ability or achievement levels. [*see also* assessment]

exceptional child A child who is either gifted or handicapped to the extent that modifications of the school's regular instructional program are necessary for the child to develop educationally to maximum potential.

fiction Works of literature which are imaginative prose narratives.

fine arts education Instruction in courses such as music, creative writing, dance, art, literature, and so on.

gifted/talented A student whose learning ability in one or more academic areas is sufficiently exceptional to require special or advanced instruction, or whose talent in a particular field is determined to be such that special or advanced training is warranted. Each state and/or school district utilizes its own criteria for defining this term, such as a minimum score on a specific I.Q. test and demonstrated academic achievement in the top three percent of students.

goals, learning The desired, broad outcomes of a child's lessons. Usually the achievement of specific knowledge and skills objectives precede achievement of learning goals.

handicapped child A child who requires special education services to enable him to reach his educational potential. Further, a child who meets one of several definitions of the handicapped (e.g., mentally retarded, emotionally disturbed, learning disabled).

health education [*see* safety/health education]

home economics Courses involving homemaker skills and sometimes parenting skills, such as cooking, sewing, nutrition awareness, child growth and development, and interior home design.

humanities Courses such as classical literature, languages, fine arts, philosophy, and others which are not considered as *the sciences*.

industrial arts Vocational courses such as woodworking, auto mechanics and metal work.

integrated curriculum A curriculum in which subject areas share goals and objectives (e.g., writing is taught/practiced in all subject areas.)

intermediate Grades four, five, and six.

junior high Grades seven and eight, and sometimes nine.

language arts Spelling, grammar, creative writing and related areas. Literature and reading are also subcategories of language arts, but are sometimes considered separately.

learning disability A malady ascribed to children assigned to special education who are not academically successful in school, do not meet the definitions of other special education categories, and whose learning problems are ostensibly not attributable to differences in language or culture.

learning style Definitions of learning style and categories of styles vary; however, we might loosely define learning styles as our individual, natural approaches to learning — involving our cognitive, affective, and physical selves. While everyone may be able to learn through all styles, each learner is most adept at learning through one or two. For example, one child may learn best kinesthetically (with body involvement), another musically, another in isolation, another through reasoning, etc.

lesson plan A teacher's written design for a lesson; usually includes one or more learning goals and/or objectives. Typically teachers write, in advance, lesson plans in each subject for an entire school week.

literature The study of writings that appear to have long-lasting, intrinsic value because of their excellence, such as fine poetry, short stories, novels, essays, and notable nonfiction works.

mathematics Courses which involve the recognition and manipulation of numbers, from counting through division, fractions, and such secondary courses as algebra, geometry, trigonometry, and calculus.

mentally retarded Children whose general intellectual functioning is in the lowest 2.5 percent of their age group as measured by an I.Q. test and who have been unable to learn expected academic and social skills. It is further necessary that these deficits are not due to cultural or linguistic differences.

music education Instruction involving music for pleasure, recognition of musical instruments, harmony, note-reading, music appreciation, and so on.

nonfiction Prose writings which deal with or offer factual information.

occupational education [*see* vocational education]

official curriculum Written learning goals and objectives, usually listed by subject area, recommended or mandated by a school district's board of education for teaching in its district.

objectives, learning Specific skills or knowledge taught to a student which he must master as a step towards a broader learning goal.

permanent file [*see* cumulative permanent record]

philosophies, educational The beliefs one has about the nature of learning, how learning should occur, how teaching should occur, learning attitudes, values that should be inherent in one's learning, learning as it relates to one's lifestyle, and so on.

physical education Courses in which students learn about and practice physical exercises, recreational games and sports, teamwork, and sportsmanship. Sometimes includes health and safety.

portfolio A file folder containing examples of a student's work and also perhaps of written assessments of his progress.

primary Grades kindergarten, one, two, and three.

progress assessment [*see* assessment]

progressive curriculum [*see* curriculum]

reading Instruction involving activities in oral communication, phonics and other means of word attack, comprehension, literature, and fluency.

remedial reading Special instruction in reading provided to children who are decidedly below average in reading ability for their age or grade placement.

safety/health education Instruction including such topics as personal hygiene, nutrition, traffic awareness, bicycle safety, poison awareness, drug awareness, sex education, and so on.

school officials Local and state school board members, state department of education administrative personnel, local school district superintendents, assistant superintendents, principals, vice principals. Some states also have county level school officials, such as a county superintendent.

school suppliers [*see* text and materials suppliers]

sciences Biology, physics, chemistry, geology, earth and space, and other common science courses.

scope and sequence chart A chart accompanying a curriculum or a textbook series which shows the sequence of learning goals and objectives or skills that are covered in the curriculum or text series.

secondary (high school) Grades nine, ten, eleven, and twelve. In some school districts grades seven and eight are also designated as *secondary*.

sequential curriculum [*see* curriculum]

social studies Courses involving history, government, geography, world cultures, current events, citizenship, and so on.

special education A program in each public school of legally-mandated educational services for students who are defined as learning handicapped (mentally retarded, emotionally disturbed, learning disabled, etc.). Special education may also include special services for gifted and talented students.

subject area/course [*see* specific subject areas] [*see* also the "K-6 Subject Area Breakdown"]

sustained curriculum [*see* curriculum]

syllabus A description of a course of instruction, including a statement of the course goals, learning objectives, the general topics covered, materials to be utilized, teacher expectations with respect to assignments, grading procedures, assignment due dates and test dates, and time periods for various other instructional activities.

teacher's manual A guidebook which accompanies a student textbook. Typically a teacher's manual will include a scope and sequence chart, specific instructions regarding how to teach the material in a particular textbook, and follow-up learning activities that complement what is covered in the textbook.

teaching method The means by which a teacher teaches a lesson. (e.g., lecture, use of manipulatives, guided exploration, direct instruction, etc.)

text and materials suppliers Companies that sell textbooks and workbooks, record forms, subject-specific equipment and materials, and other school products. These companies vary in size and may support one or more curricular areas. Some cater exclusively to the needs of home-schooling parents.

textbook series A series of books in one subject area, one text for each ability level or grade level, published by a single publishing company. Students progress from text to text as they move from level to level.

the writing process A procedure for writing which includes prewriting activities (firsthand or secondhand experience with a topic, thought, discussion), rough writing, revising, editing, final writing, and "publication."

unit of study A segment of a subject, course, or subject-area textbook which is covered separately from, but in some logical sequence with, other segments. An American history textbook, for example, may be segmented into chronological units covering Native American history, European discovery of the "new continent," early white settlements, the Revolutionary War, and so on.

vocational education Courses intended to prepare students to enter vocations. These often include business courses, industrial arts courses, and homemaker courses.

PHOTOCOPY MASTERS

Worksheet 1 My Educational Philosophies

Worksheet 2 Lifelong Aims of My Child's Education

File Copy A My Educational Philosophies and the
Lifelong Aims of My Child's Education

Worksheet 3 My Child

Worksheet 4 Requirements and Choices

File Copy B My Child's Home-School Subjects

Worksheet 5 Rough Copy Curriculum Sheet

Worksheet 6 Texts and Materials Evaluation

File Copy C The Textbooks and Materials I Will Use to
Teach My Child's Curriculum

Worksheet 1
My Educational Philosophies

1. I believe my child's learning attitude should be:

2. I believe my child's learning should lead towards this kind of lifestyle:

3. I believe the following basic values should be integrated into my child's curriculum:

4. How I believe children learn best:

5. How I believe teachers teach best:

6. My other educational philosophies:

Worksheet 2
Lifelong Aims of My Child's Education

My child's curriculum year-by-year should enable him or her to:

1. _____

2. _____

3. _____

4. _____

5. _____

6. _____

7. _____

8. _____

9. _____

10. _____

11. _____

12. _____

13. _____

14. _____

15. _____

16. _____

17. _____

18. _____

File Copy A

My Educational Philosophies and the Lifelong Aims of My Child's Education

Statement of My Educational Philosophies:

_____

_____

_____

_____

_____

_____

_____

_____

_____

_____

_____

Lifelong Aims of My Child's Education:

1. _____

2. _____

3. _____

4. _____

5. _____

6. _____

7. _____

8. _____

9. _____

10. _____

11. _____

12. _____

Worksheet 3
My Child

Child's name _____ Age _____ Birthdate _____

Grade level _____   How I determined grade level:

My child's academic interests, both general and specific:

My child's academic abilities:

My child's special learning needs:

Any learner labels that have been attached to my child by school personnel:

How do school records describe my child's deficiencies, difficulties, special needs, and/or special talents:

My child's learning styles:

Worksheet 4
Requirements and Choices

Required Subjects for Home Schoolers in My State	Subjects I Noted in Sample Curriculums or in the "Typical Grade-Level Subjects" Roster	Other Subjects I Want to Teach or That My Child Wants to Study

Notes:

My Child's Home-School Subjects

1. _____

2. _____

3. _____

4. _____

5. _____

6. _____

7. _____

8. _____

9. _____

10. _____

11. _____

Worksheet 5
Rough Copy Curriculum Sheet

Subject: _____

Goals	Objectives
The student will be able to:	The student will be able to:
1.	1.1.
	1.2.
	1.3.
	1.4
2.	2.1.
	2.2.
	2.3
	2.4
3.	3.1
	3.2
	3.3
	3.4
4.	4.1
	4.2
	4.3
	4.4
5.	5.1
	5.2
	5.3
	5.4

Worksheet 6
Texts and Materials Evaluation

Subject:_____

	Text/Material Title	Supplier Address and Price	My Evaluation
1.			
2.			
3.			
4.			
5.			

File Copy C

THE TEXTBOOKS AND MATERIALS
I WILL USE TO TEACH MY CHILD'S CURRICULUM

Subject:_____   Texts/Materials:

Subject:_____   Texts/Materials:

Subject:_____   Texts/Materials:

Subject:_____   Texts/Materials:

Subject:_____   Texts/Materials:

Subject:_____   Texts/Materials:

Subject:_____   Texts/Materials:

Subject:_____   Texts/Materials:

Subject:_____   Texts/Materials:

Subject:_____   Texts/Materials:

Subject:_____   Texts/Materials:

Our Basic Reference Library

_____   _____

_____   _____

_____   _____

INDEX OF WORKSHEETS, FILE COPIES, SAMPLES AND ROSTERS

General Index